a shetland cook book

jenni simmons

First published 1978
© Jenni Simmons, 1978

This edition printed and published by
The Shetland Times Ltd.
Prince Alfred Street, Lerwick, Shetland

The Ifland of Shetland, lying between the fixtieth and fixty-firft Degree of Latitude, which is chiefly mountainous, affording good Pafturage, but beholden to the Isles of Orkney for Corn. The Air cold and piercing, and fubject to fuch tempeftuous Seas, that during the Winter Seafon, they neither correfpond with, nor hear anything concerning the reft of Mankind inhabiting the other parts of the Globe; the People nevertheless arrive here to great Ages; the Difeafe chiefly afflicting them is the Scurvy, occafioned by being too much confined to eating Salt-fifh. They have like-wife a Diftemper, chiefly among the poorer Sort, occafioned by the Want of Bread, by which they live almoft wholly on Fifh for feveral Months together . . .

quantities

Solid	ounces (ozs)	grams (g)
1 teaspoon (tsp)	¼	8
1 dessertspoon (dsp)	½	15
1 tablespoon (tbsp) and fat size of an egg	1	30
knob of fat	2	60
1 teacup	4	120
1 breakfastcup	8	240
1 teacup + 1 breakfastcup	12	360
2 breakfastcup	1 pound (lb)	480 (½ kilo)
4 breakfastcup	2 lb	1 k.

Liquid	pints	litres (l)
1 teacupful (or 8 tbsp)	¼	.125 (1/8 l)
1 breakfastcupful	½	.25
2 breakfastcupful	1	.5
4 breakfastcupful	2	1

oven temperatures

Description	Gas	Electricity °f	°c
very slow or warm	¼ or ½	250	130
slow	2	300	150
fairly hot or bright	3	325	170
moderate or good	4-6	380	190
quick or smart	7	425	220
hot	8	450	230
very hot	10	480	240

meat

BEEF

The hairst, when winter is not far away, was the traditional time for selling or slaughtering the unwanted beasts. Every carcass was well hung before the cutting up, the 'breaking down of a cow'.

A whole cow would be shared between several families, or perhaps one family took a quarter animal. Nothing was wasted. Shetland beef is fine flavoured and tender, but it was seldom eaten fresh: some might be dried and salted — blawn maet — although salt was very expensive. Unsalted, dried beef ('very insipid stuff') is eaten boiled, with vegetables cooked in the same pot.

To roast: never put salt on the meat as this draws out the juice and makes it dry. Never cook beef with mutton dripping (pork dripping can be used as it will not affect the flavour). Set in the top (hottest part) of the oven first. Baste often, at least every ten minutes. Allow 15 mins per lb meat plus 15-30 mins extra, depending on the heat of the oven. Just before the meat is done, shake a little flour over, baste and return to the top of the oven for a final 5 mins. If the fat is poured off into a bowl with a little cold water in it, then it will lift off like a cake when cold.

Roast beef is not traditional. In fact roasting was thought a wasteful method; it takes up a good fire, and the meat will shrink.

1

There are great Numbers of Crows, Hawks, and Eagles, Fheep and Lambs in this Ifland; the Horfes are fo remarkably fmall and light as to be lifted up by a fingle Man, and yet fo ftrong af to carry double . . .

mince

Cook the mince very slowly in a little water, keeping it unbroken in the pot. When the mince is ready (test with a knife) pour over a thick gravy mixture of 1 tbsp gravy flour to 1 breakfastcupful water and cook through the meat, stirring it in with a fork. Eat with chappit tatties (page 55).

sassermaet

(Sausagemeat)

For 6 lbs minced beef:
1 tsp allspice
1 tsp black pepper
1 tsp white pepper
1 tsp ground cloves
½ tsp Jamaica pepper
½ tsp cinnamon
3 ozs salt

Mix all the spices with the salt first, then stir through the minced meat very well.

A Shetland word for salt is britrack.

brönies

Mix sassermaet and minced steak in equal quantities. Add breadcrumbs, chopped onion, seasoning and an egg to bind the meat together. Mix by hand and make into cakes a good inch thick. Fry in smoking fat, both sides, then reduce the heat and cook more slowly until ready. Drain off fat. Delicious tucked into a warm bannock (page 50).

a simple meat pudding

Fill a greased pudding bowl nearly to the top with mince. Cover with buttered paper (or cooking foil) and set in a pan of water. Steam 1 hour. Turn out of bowl after a few minutes and serve with a thick gravy (page 17).

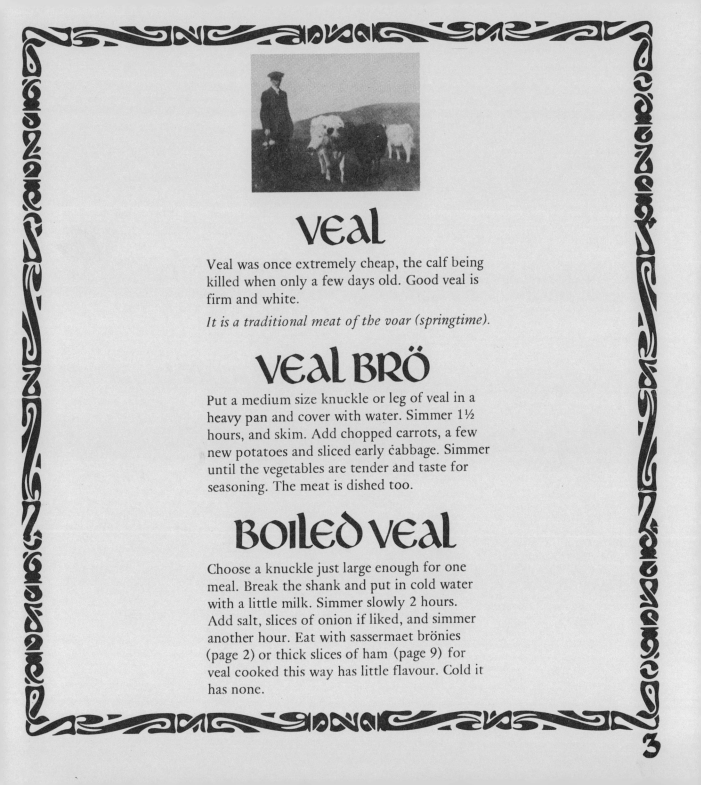

veal

Veal was once extremely cheap, the calf being killed when only a few days old. Good veal is firm and white.

It is a traditional meat of the voar (springtime).

veal Brö

Put a medium size knuckle or leg of veal in a heavy pan and cover with water. Simmer 1½ hours, and skim. Add chopped carrots, a few new potatoes and sliced early cabbage. Simmer until the vegetables are tender and taste for seasoning. The meat is dished too.

Boiled veal

Choose a knuckle just large enough for one meal. Break the shank and put in cold water with a little milk. Simmer slowly 2 hours. Add salt, slices of onion if liked, and simmer another hour. Eat with sassermaet brönies (page 2) or thick slices of ham (page 9) for veal cooked this way has little flavour. Cold it has none.

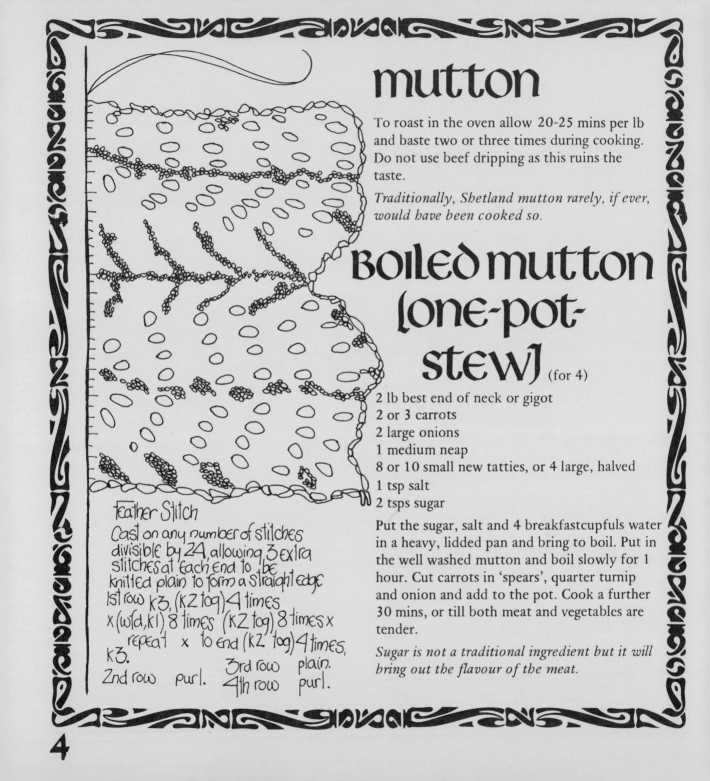

mutton

To roast in the oven allow 20-25 mins per lb and baste two or three times during cooking. Do not use beef dripping as this ruins the taste.

Traditionally, Shetland mutton rarely, if ever, would have been cooked so.

boiled mutton (one-pot-stew) (for 4)

2 lb best end of neck or gigot
2 or 3 carrots
2 large onions
1 medium neap
8 or 10 small new tatties, or 4 large, halved
1 tsp salt
2 tsps sugar

Put the sugar, salt and 4 breakfastcupfuls water in a heavy, lidded pan and bring to boil. Put in the well washed mutton and boil slowly for 1 hour. Cut carrots in 'spears', quarter turnip and onion and add to the pot. Cook a further 30 mins, or till both meat and vegetables are tender.

Sugar is not a traditional ingredient but it will bring out the flavour of the meat.

Feather Stitch
Cast on any number of stitches divisible by 24, allowing 3 extra stitches at each end to be knitted plain to form a straight edge
1st row k3, (k2 tog) 4 times
x (wfd, k1) 8 times (k2 tog) 8 times x
repeat x to end (k2 tog) 4 times, k3.
2nd row purl. 3rd row plain. 4th row purl.

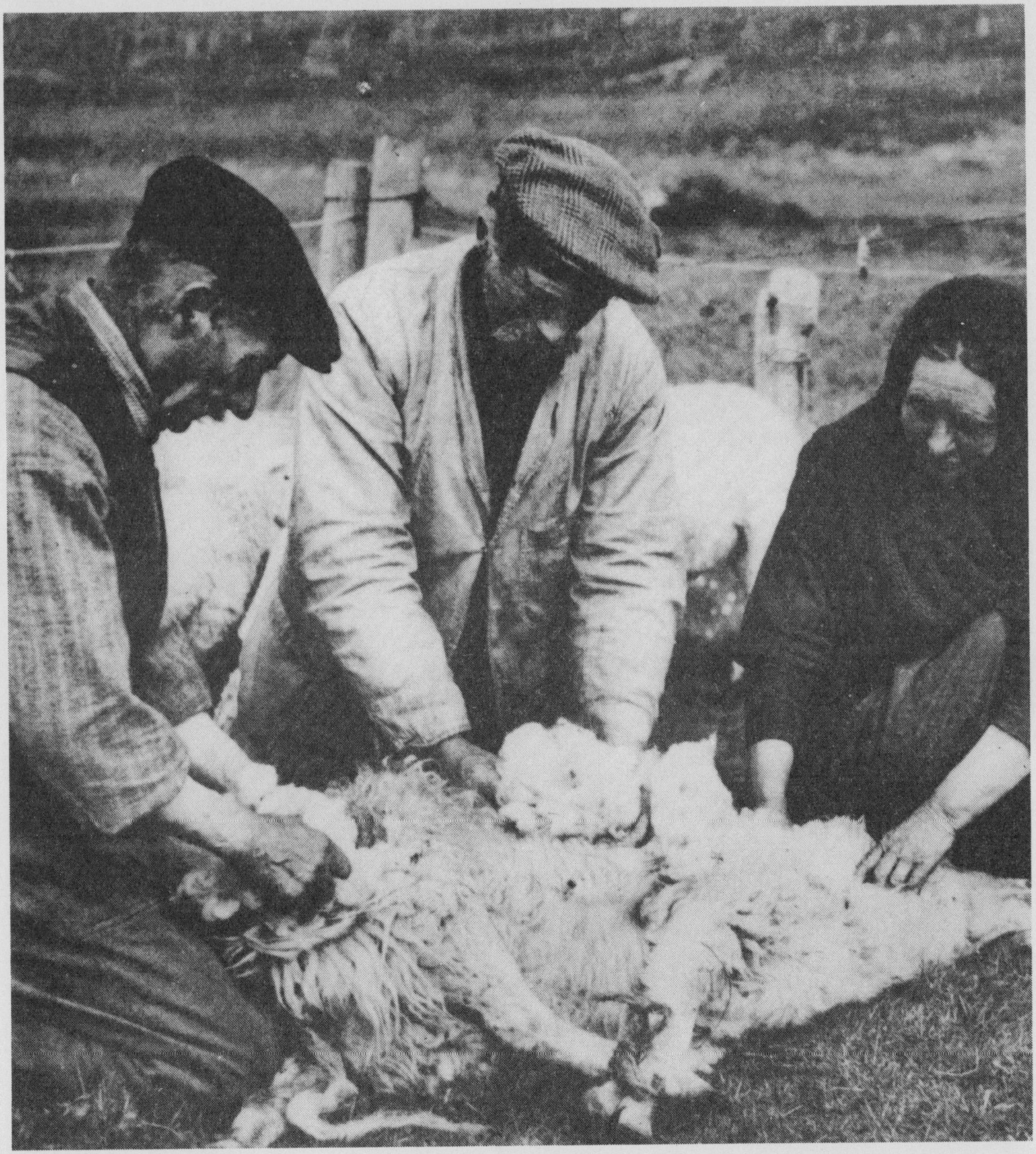

The Sheep too are small, but their wool so fine as that a pair of stockings made of it will pass thro' a common gold ring.

reested mutton

The mutton is first salted, then hung and dried in the roof by the fire: the peat reek gives a unique smokey flavour to the mutton tee.

The veggil is where the meat is hung to reest.

vivda

Vivda is mutton dried by the wind, not salt. Its flavour is greatly to be esteemed, the meat being cut in very fine slices.

The meat was hung in a skjeo (a stone larder built so that air could blow freely through the walls).

sheep's heed brö

A sweed heed (singed sheep's head) — split
1 teacup fine oatmeal
salt and pepper
carrot
onion or leeks
turnip

Clean the head well, particularly the mouth and nostrils. Soak in salt and water 4 hours, then remove and tie together in its original shape. Have a large panful of boiling water ready and put in the head. Boil gently 1½ hours then lift out (allow all the water to drain back into the pan first). Skim the pot with a metal spoon. Add vegetables, chopped, with the oatmeal and simmer a further 30 mins.

BOILED SAAT MUTTON (for 6)

2 lb salt meat
1 lb carrot, sliced
pinch pepper
1 lb potatoes, cut small
1 large onion, sliced

Wash meat and cook in 1 breakfastcupful water for 1 hour. Then remove, and cut in small pieces and return to the pot. Add vegetables and seasoning and simmer 1 hour. This can be done in a casserole (or lidded dish) in a slow oven. Cook for 2 hours.

LAMB (OR CALF) SWEETBREAD

1 sweetbread from the throat or heart
1 teacupful stock

Steep sweetbread 1 hour and bring to boil in cold water. Boil 5 mins. Drain and skin. Add stock and seasoning. Simmer 1 hour. Pour thin cream over before dishing.   (for 2)

Swine of a small kind . . . might be much more numerous than they are, but, being found very hurtful in turning up and spoiling the grass . . . the people are restricted by a country act to such a small number proportionable to the land they labour, which they must not exceed.

BOILED PORK

Allow 30 mins per lb (plus 20 mins if under 5 lbs). Salt cured pork must be soaked at least 12 hours. Put ham in cold water to cover and bring to boil. Add a teacup of brown sugar for extra flavour. Keep gently boiling throughout. Cool in the liquid overnight. Next day cut off the skin and then dust over with wholemeal flour. Save the cooking liquid as a stock for soup.

PORK

Pork should always be well cooked. To roast: score the skin with a sharp knife with lines about ½" apart. Cover in well-greased paper (or put in a roastabag with a large piece of lard dripping). Cook on the lowest rack in a smart oven, allowing 30 mins for each lb of pork plus 25 mins. Baste frequently, removing paper to do so. After the last baste pour a little clear honey over the skin and return to the the oven — this time to the highest rack — to make a delicious crackling. Try with gooseberry sauce (page 65).

Roasting would most often have been done over a red fire.

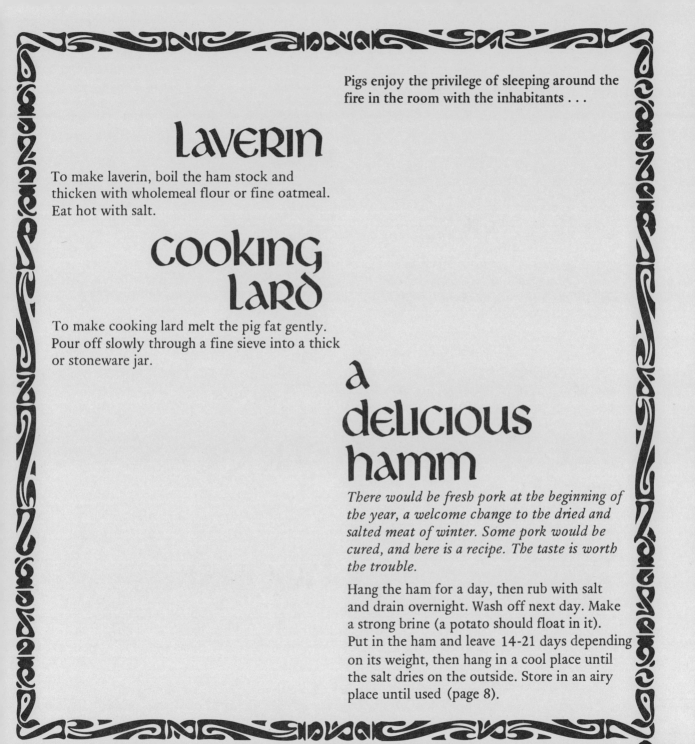

Pigs enjoy the privilege of sleeping around the fire in the room with the inhabitants . . .

LAVERIN

To make laverin, boil the ham stock and thicken with wholemeal flour or fine oatmeal. Eat hot with salt.

COOKING LARD

To make cooking lard melt the pig fat gently. Pour off slowly through a fine sieve into a thick or stoneware jar.

A DELICIOUS HAMM

There would be fresh pork at the beginning of the year, a welcome change to the dried and salted meat of winter. Some pork would be cured, and here is a recipe. The taste is worth the trouble.

Hang the ham for a day, then rub with salt and drain overnight. Wash off next day. Make a strong brine (a potato should float in it). Put in the ham and leave 14-21 days depending on its weight, then hang in a cool place until the salt dries on the outside. Store in an airy place until used (page 8).

I mind when I wis young, we'd hae mebbe hauf a koo an' we'd mak sassermaet, puddens to hang idda roef . . . an' I wid wash da faa an' pak it fu wi a mixtur o' floor, o'tmel, suet (no the Atora), saat, sultanas, currn's, twa'er tree raisn's wi a pinch o' cinnamon an' bakin' soda . . . hoo much . . . waal, dat depens on jus whit wis wanted . . .

puddings

Each Martinmas the croft animals which were not to be sold or kept through the winter were killed. This happened every year, until the end of the last century. Puddings are a traditional way of not letting anything go to waste. Made and stored in the roof they were a careful provision against winter hunger.

Pudding skins can be had from butchers in Shetland. First soak in brine overnight, clean under a running tap and cut into lengths. Do not overfill, as some space is needed to allow for cooking, then twist and knot the ends.

mellie pudden

Mellie pudden is made of oatmeal as a base with chopped or minced suet, flour, salt and pepper and fine-chopped onion (if liked). Mix all the ingredients by hand, fill the pudding skins and prick before boiling in salted water. They keep once cooked, but store in a cool place. Good sliced or fried whole.

spaarls

Spaarls are puddings made from any meat scraps, well minced, with oatmeal. Season well. They can be stewed in water.

Not traditional, but very good, is to eat them sliced in a thick, rich gravy (page 17).

burstin puddings

Traditionally made with burstin, a fine meal made from roasted bere, hand ground.

Mix bere meal with pig lard and a little salt.

hoonska

The pudding which is black with cooked blood, flour and suet. Prick the skins before boiling, or deep fry, rolled first in beaten egg and then fine oatmeal.

It is traditional to use ox blood.

A 19th century tradition was to bleed the cows once or twice a year. The blood was boiled and thickened with oatmeal, eaten with a little milk.

This was food I did not admire.

curny pudding

Makes a good breakfast on Shetland winter days. Mix fine oatmeal and flour in equal quantities. Add chopped suet to currants and/or sultanas which have been soaked overnight in water (to make the fruit more juicy). Pack a sheep's stomach which has been well soaked in salted water and cleaned, stitch up and boil. Once cooked, rub the pudding with fine oatmeal. Delicious fried in thick slices with bacon.

This pudding is too rich to be traditional fare.

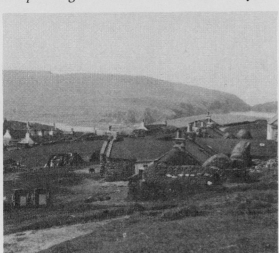

penshens

(tripe, cow's stomach)

If not prepared, wash well and scrape clean. Put in pan with cold water and boil up. Then pour off, cover again with cold water and re-boil. Do this several times. When cold, put in fresh water and simmer 6 or 7 hours. Keep covered with water all the time. When cooked, cool overnight in the cooking liquid.

(for 4 or 5)

2 lb tripe, prepared
knob of butter
salt and pepper

Wash and dry tripe, put in a buttered roasting tin and spread with butter. Bake in a slow oven for 2 hours. Baste often, using more butter if needed. Eat with chappit tatties (page 55), and a thick beef gravy, using stock or a beef cube and wholemeal flour.

seal

Seal were caught for their oil and skins. The islanders of Unst sold the seal skin but salted the meat. It eats like venison.

. . I have, however, seen some of the poorer sort eat them.

11

fowl

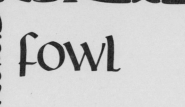

black pot

chicken

Singe fowl and rub over with a cloth. Wash well and clean innards. Dry. By hand, mix 1 breakfastcup breadcrumbs, 1 teacup sausagemeat and salt and pepper. Add a beaten egg to bind. Stuff well the body of the fowl, fastening neck and legs to keep it in.

To roast: put fowl with fat and a large cup of boiling water in roasting tin and cover with paper spread thick with fat. The time taken depends on the age of the fowl.

To stew: first cut off legs at knee, then put in a stew pan with a little hot fat, to brown over. Pour in 1 teacupful water and cook till tender. Keep adding a little water and turn fowl whilst cooking. A gravy can be made from the cooking liquid.

goose

At one time geese were kept in great number, for their feathers.

Goose is in season from September until Christmas. In March the young green geese come into season. A goose should not be eaten when more than a year old (the feet of an old goose are red). A full grown goose should hang for a week before cooking.

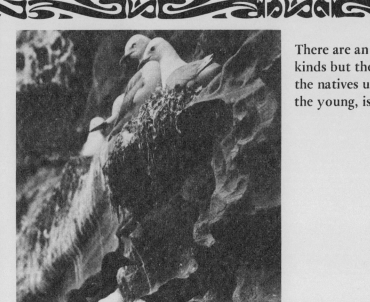

There are an abundance of seafowls of various kinds but there flesh is blackish . . . the method the natives use in taking the eggs, or catching the young, is a very dangerous one . . .

stuffed duck

Singe, pick clean and wash well in cold water. Then fill body with duck stuffing. For this take:

1 breakfastcup grated bread
2 good sized onions, peeled and chopped
butter (or egg) and milk to bind

Parboil the duck for 30 mins in a deep pan then put in roasting tin with fat and a little water. Baste often.

reested goose

A goose is plucked, drawn and salted for a few days, then hung to reest in the peat smoke.

seafowl

At one time it was a seasonal event for the craigsmen to gather eggs in large quantities. The eggs were hard boiled, to keep, and the seafowl cooked in the grudack (a large pot).

scarf (Shag)

Eaten on Foula and the outlying islands. They have a fishy taste.

lomvie (Guillemot)

Caught on the cliffs. The hen is a foolish bird, and great numbers were taken, by the neck with nooses made from hair.

13

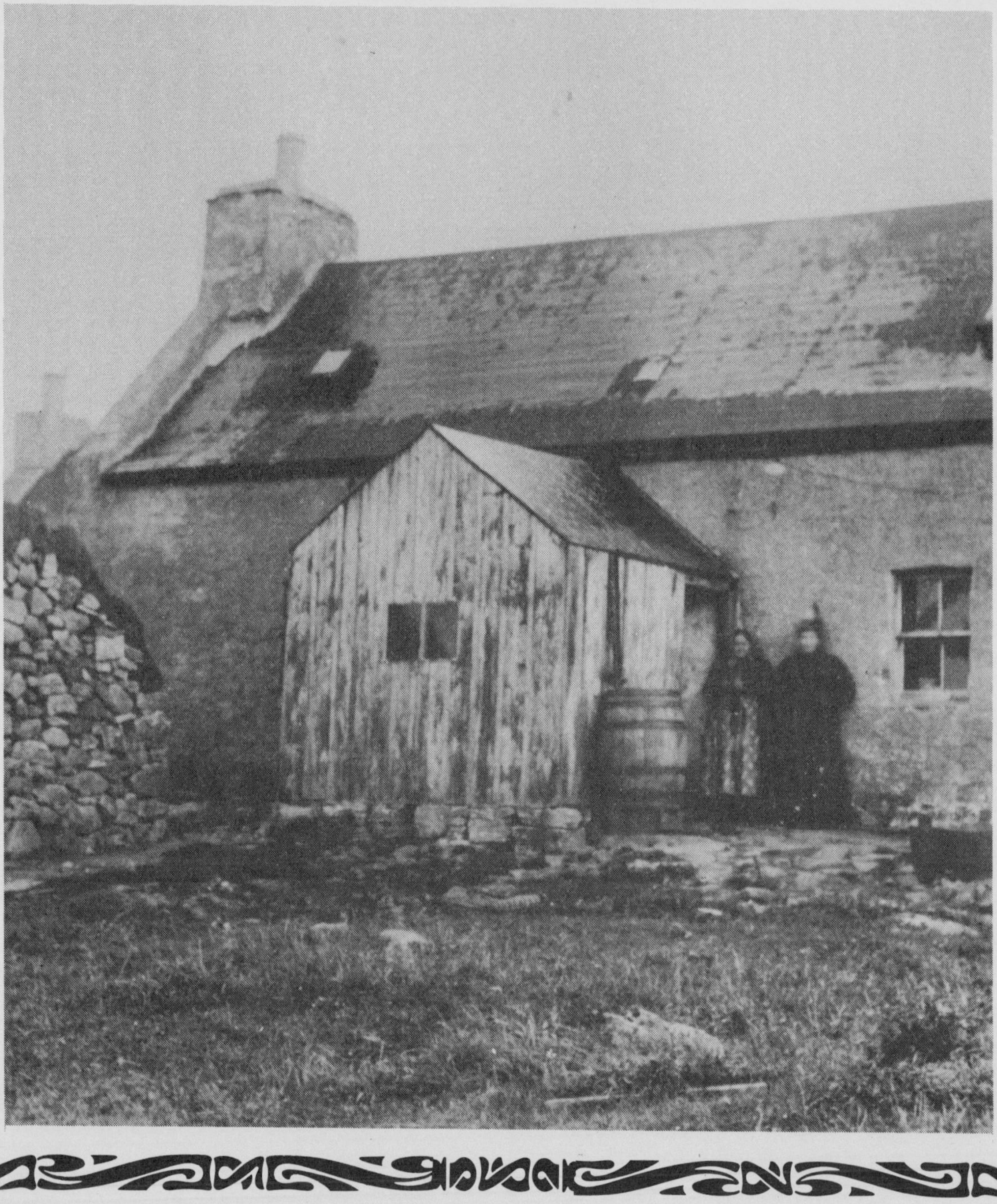

dunter

(Eider duck)

The feathers and down are used for pillows
and quilt covers. Cook only the breast and legs.
Use a stew pan to brown the joints in hot fat,
then cover with water and simmer until tender.

stock-duik

(Mallard)

Mallard nest in Shetland. If it is an old bird,
first fry quickly in hot fat, turning it on all sides
sides. Then add cold water to cover with
slices of fat bacon. Stew gently. Otherwise,
roast with duck stuffing.

GAME

Rabbit

A good rabbit will feed 6. Soak the skinned rabbit in salted water for 15 mins. Clean out well, removing heart and liver and cut off the head. Divide into joints (the legs make one joint each) and rub with flour. Heat lard or dripping in a stew pan till it smokes, then put in the rabbit joints and fry briskly. Make sure that each joint is sealed with the hot fat all round. Add slices of onion, if liked, with the heart and liver, chopped. Season well, cover with water and a lid and leave to stew slowly. Eat with a **thick gravy**: heat a knob of butter and add a tablespoon of wholemeal flour with a teaspoon of gravy flour. All the butter should be taken up. Then add a breakfastcupful of water, slowly. Stir all the time and cook gently till thick. Add salt and pepper. Try adding a dash of sherry, too. Rabbit eats very with rowan jelly (page 64).

It is always in season save at the breeding time.

hare

Hare is best between October and February. If it is young the teeth will be white. A hare is very large and can feed 8 or 10.

Wash the skinned hare and leave to soak in cold salt water 1 hour together with heart and liver. Joint. Put in a pan with seasoning and cover with water. Simmer until tender, skimming off the fat. Take out hare. Heat a knob of butter and cook 1 tablespoon of flour in it, stirring. Then add the stock from the pan, pouring it through a sieve. Let it boil 10 mins and then pour over hare. Try with bilberry (page 64) and sassermaet brönies (page 2).

Neither rabbit nor hare are traditional eating, but both are good for the pot.

17

. . . they are moft remarkably dextrous and nimble in climbing the Rocks; this Art they are under a Neceffity of putting in practice, to obtain the Fea-Fowl and their Eggs, which are no inconfiderable Part of their Fupport . . .

fish

Every man has a sea loch at his door: and the poorest can have a meal of fish for putting his line in it.

ish is best eaten as soon as it is got. If this is not possible, keep very cold or in a cloth dipped in vinegar.

Traditional Shetland ways of keeping fish are to reest by the peat fire (reeklins are strips of fish dried in the smoke); to gozen (dry un-salted, in the sun) or to dry, unsalted, in the wind (blawn fish). A fish wind and sun dried is sookit. Strings of salted fish hang on the gavel until they gadder a bloom (glisten with salt.)

PREPARING fish to cook

Wash all sea fish in salt water and rub with salt to remove any blood.

To gut, put the fish on layers of newspaper (throw away as necessary). Slit down the stomach of the fish from head and take out intestines, roe and liver. If haddock or mackerel, make a cut at the base of the head and break it off backwards, then all the intestines will come out together. If a flat fish, make a wide slit on the darker side below the gills and remove intestines. To scale, pour over a little boiling water, then scrape with a knife from head to tail. Hold the knife at an angle to the fish.

ways to cook fish

If frying, lard can be used but cooking oil will give a better taste to the fish. White fish should be fried in oil and butter mixed. First soak 5 mins in salted milk.

To stuff, slit fish along the backbone, then cut this at each end and take away. Keep the stuffing in by wrapping fish in oiled greaseproof paper and tie round with string or use cooking foil.

If cooking in water, never let the fish boil fast. Always bring up to the boil and keep at simmer point. Cover the fish completely with water and add vinegar to keep the flesh white. (Do not add vinegar to pink-fleshed fish). Cod, hake and ling need 20 mins per lb. Halibut or turbot need 30 mins per lb. Whole fish (or large pieces) should be put in cold water and brought to simmer point but fillets of fish should go into boiling water and the heat reduced.

Before the potato was grown in Shetland dried fish was pounded to make a flour for baking.

a simple fish soup (for 4)

1 cod head
½ lb. white fish
1 tsp. salt
2 sliced carrots
1 chopped onion or leek
1 teacupful milk

Put fish in a deep heavy pan and cover with salted water. Simmer 1 hour, adding the vegetables after 30 mins cooking. Lastly add the milk hot.

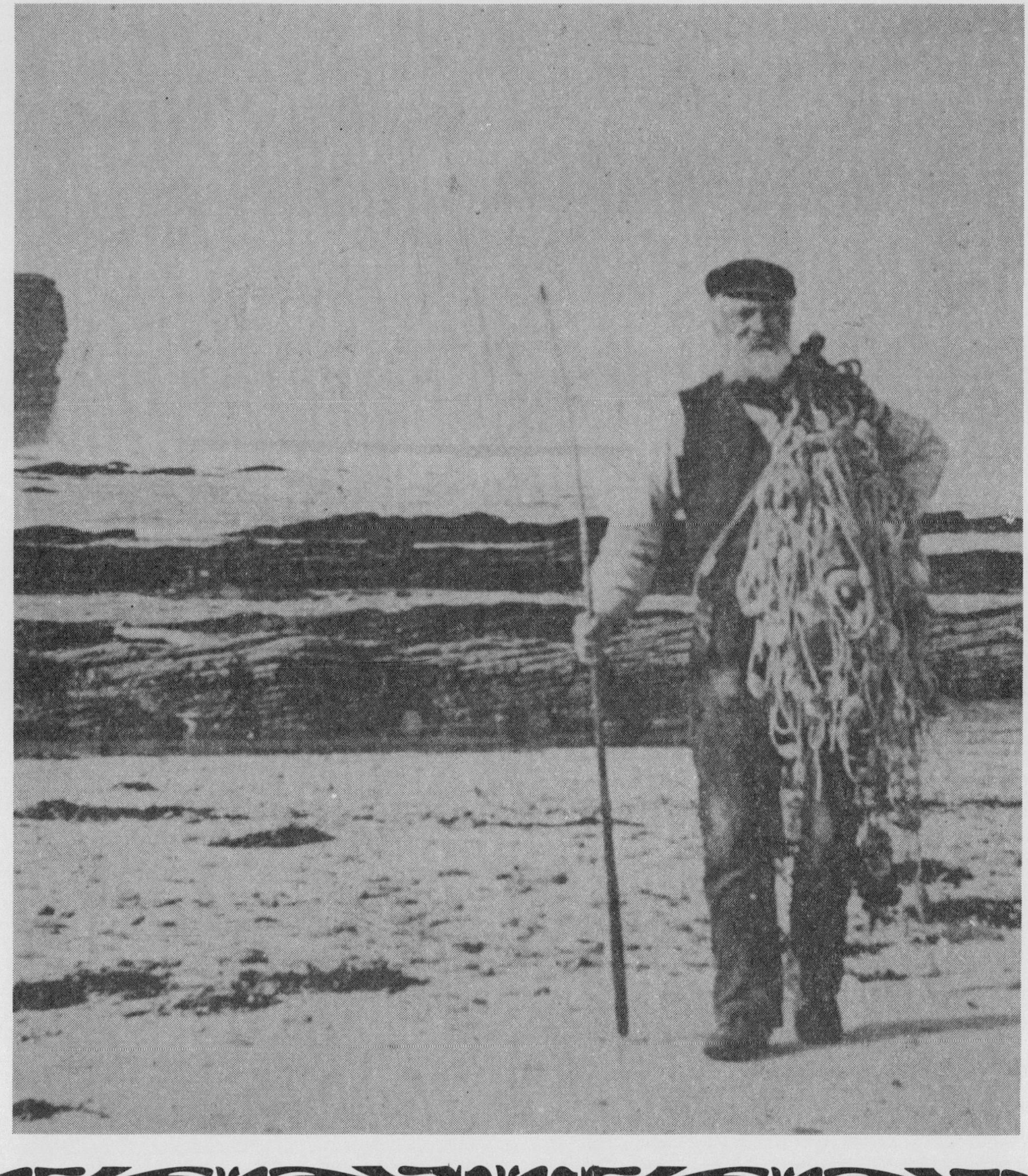

saithe

(coal fish) are caught all year round.

Often shoals of the very young fish are so thick in winter voes that a bucket is easily filled. The older fish (ruthin, 3-year old, drulyan, 4-year old or skoorie, mature fish) are caught in open sea. Piltaks and sillocks can be caught by waand (rod) or poke net at the craigs.

sillock

(very young saithe)

piltak

(2-year old saithe)

Roast the fish whole, with its liver inside, skewered. This is mougildin or spiolkin. Delicious with boiled tatties. Eat very hot.

The sillock provided a good meal for large families: it was 'the principal food of the poorer classes' well into the 19th century.

Boiled piltak

Gut and clean. Cook whole in water that just turns in the pan till the flesh begins to flake. Drain well. Eat cold, with salt and pepper and buttered bannocks (page 50) or cold tatties. and a glass of milk. A traditional Shetland supper.

saide an gree

Simmer the fish with the liver. As the gree (oil) rises to the top, skim off, keep hot and use as a sauce over the fish. Needs plenty of tatties.

Maks a fine deenin (a good full meal).

krampies

Boil the sillock livers in a little water and drain.

Traditionally they are mixed with burstin (roasted ground bere) and eaten whilst still hot.

krappin

Make a stuffing with bere meal (or fine oatmeal) and flour mixed in equal quantities, salt and pepper. Add sufficient fish liver to bind.

Traditionally, the stuffing is packed into washed fish heads, gills removed, and boiled in well salted water. These are krappit heeds.

Try making dumplings from the mixture. They can be cooked in boiling salt water, or atop a fish soup or stew.

muggie

This is the fish stomach. Cleaned it can be stuffed with fish liver, oatmeal and salt to make krappit muggies. Boil very gently. Eat with boiled cabbage (page 56) well buttered.

haakamuggie

Clean the fish stomach without tearing. Stuff with a hash of flaked fish, sounds and livers. Simmer. Serve in a bowl with some of the cooking liquid spooned over, and eat with bere bannocks (page 46).

liver-flaakies

are traditionally made with piltaks not completely dried. Split two, removing backbones. Then 'sandwich' the piltaks with fresh fish liver. Wrap in cooking foil and bake slow.

Flaakies were set on the hearthstone, to roast by the fire.

liver-krüs

Make a stiff dough with wholemeal flour and water only. A little bere meal or oatmeal may be added. Knead into the shape of a cup or krüs, making the base flat. Save a little of the dough. Fill the cup with fish livers and use strips of the remaining dough to make a lattice over the top. Set the krüs on a greased baking sheet. Use the middle rack of a fairly hot oven.

Traditionally the krüs would bake on the hearth: the pastry makes both the dish and the meal.

23

. . . the women found work baiting haddock
lines for their family . . .

LIVER BANNOCKS

Make a bannock mixture (page   as for braand-iron bannocks) but do not add any lard. Lightly fork in the uncooked livers. Put on an ungreased tin and bake in a hot oven until well risen. Eat on their own or with fish instead of tatties.

Always use fish livers very fresh: it is best to buy them for eating the same day.

They eat exceedingly well.

A pannabrad is a little pot for melting fish livers in. The oil was used in lamps.

RIZZARED HADDOCK

Skin and split fish and flour well. Eat with plenty of butter.

Traditionally this is toasted at the fire till brown.

SKUED HADDOCK

Wash and skin fish and put in a heavy pan. Cover with water and add a knob of butter. Simmer. Mix a little seasoned flour with milk or water and pour over the fish, cooking gently till thick. Hake can be cooked in this way also.

STAPP

This is a mixture of boiled fish with the boiled livers forked in. Eat hot, with a knob of butter and pepper. With krappin (page 23) it is a tradition.

The chief fishery was the deep-sea or haaf fishing (so called from the Old Norse haf, ocean) for ling, tusk, and cod, prosecuted at a considerable distance from the land in large, open six-oared boats, called sixerns.

Sometimes the highest land would be dipping to meet the sea before lines were set. Their only compass was the moder-di, the under-swell that always sets toward land whatever the airt of the wind. The four'areen (four oared boats) generally returned each night with their catch.

whiting

Eat as fresh as can be. It is a dry fish. Open down the back and bone, or clean and cook whole, scoring first with a knife. Coat in flour and fry gold brown. Then melt a good piece of butter in the pan with the juice of half a lemon and pour over fish while it is still frothy.

kiossed heeds

These are fish heads or small fish rolled in a cloth and left in an airy place (between the stones of a wall) till gamey. Then boil and eat with butter and tatties.

laiger

Laiger (halibut) are scarce now in Shetland waters. Once so numerous and worthless 'they were used as linns to make the beaching of a sixern less laborious'. The laiger is a solid fish; 4 ozs will make a good helping. Cook by poaching gently in water to cover. Eat with melted butter.

A baar is the long, side cut of a laiger, including the fin. But the long cut from its back or belly is a lengie. Broe is its liver. The halibut is sometimes called a turbot or turbot-fluke.

millfish

Millfish (turbot) are sold in large pieces. Do not buy any that are bluey. Scrub the skin with salt. If cooking the fish whole, slit down the backbone first. The thick fins are cooked too. Put the fish in a buttered, heavy pan or lidded dish in the oven with chopped carrot, onion and a handful of tatties, in a little water. Season. Simmer, basting from time to time. Allow 12 mins per lb.

Another name for the turbot is the quern fish, from its shape.

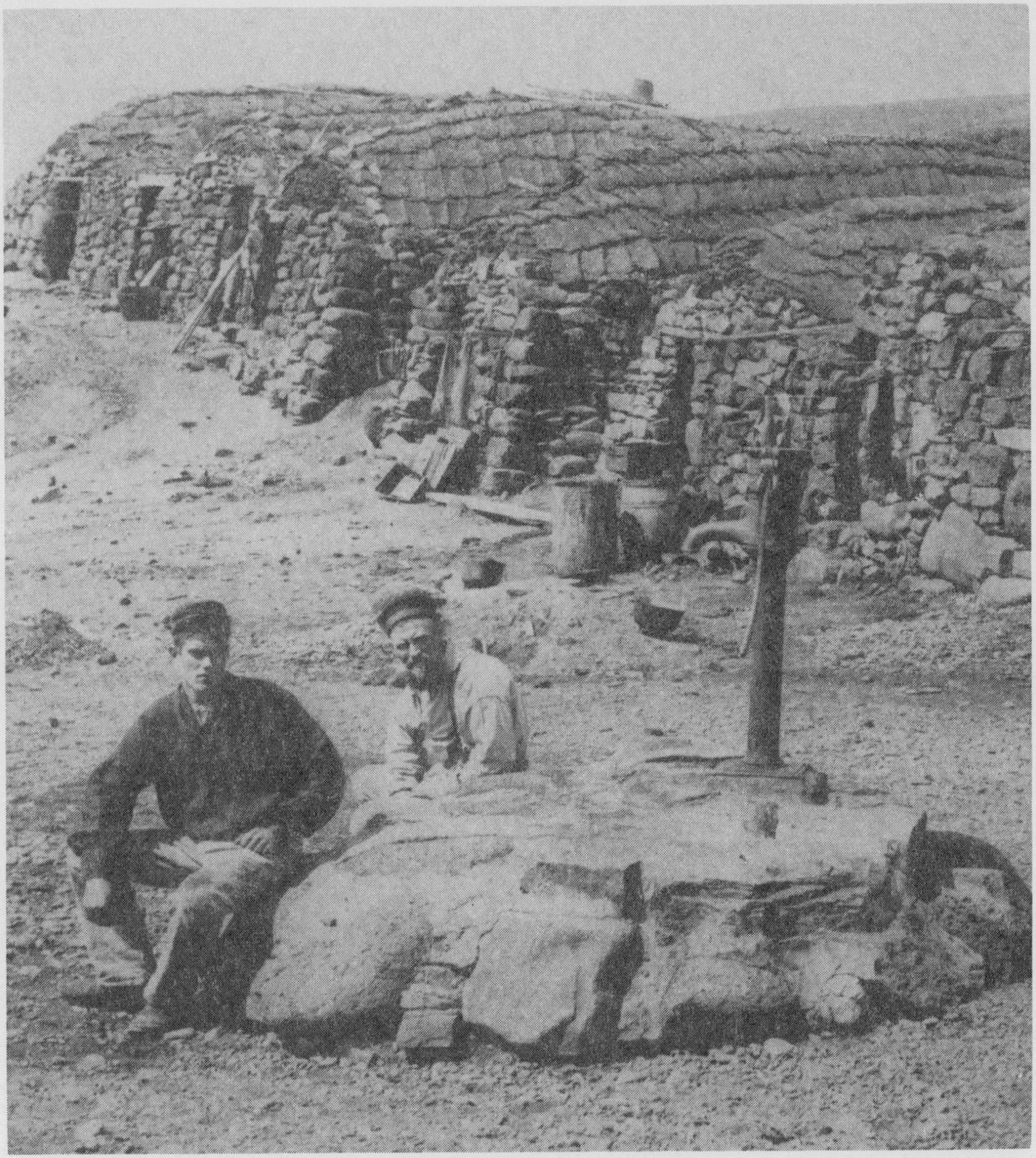

cod

oh for a red waur codlin....

A rich cod ground was discovered off Foula at the beginning of the 19th century and named Regent's Bank. Grounds at Rockall and off Faroe were fished, the nearer banks abandoned, and boats were specially fitted out for deep sea cod fishing. The little fleet was unique in Scotland, sailing in the late 1840's as far as the Davis Straits. By the end of the century it had all but disappeared.

When buying, pick the tail steak as most tender or if whole, choose a short fat fish, a stablin cod, as the best eating. Now both cod and ling are little fished from Shetland. Torsk (tusk) can be cooked like cod.

A Shetland word for tusk is brismik.

Boiled cod

Before cooking, wash, dry and sprinkle with salt. Stand 30 mins. Dry again. Let the water simmer very gently when the fish is cooking. When done the flesh will move away from the bone.

During the Winter, or Spring Seasons, in many parts of the country, they take amazing quantities of Cod . . . This is a great help to the poor people, as the catching of them is attended with little or no danger . . .

to salt cod before boiling

Remove head and backbone but leave belly uncut. Clean well. Rub coarse (sea) salt over and put salt side down on a board. Put more salt on the top of the fish and cover. Leave in a cold place 48 hours, wipe the fish well, replace on board and weight. Leave 2 hours, then wash and cut into thick slices. Put into boiling water, then simmer.

salt cod

Soak in 6 or 8 changes of water at least 24 hours (use rainwater). Drain, skin and remove bones. Simmer 15-20 mins. If buying salt cod choose only fillets which are thick and white (yellow ones are not fresh).

cod rhans

Wash roe and tie in muslin (it breaks easily during cooking). Cover and simmer 30 mins. Skin when still warm. If the rhans are peerie fry in butter for a few minutes only and eat hot.

slott

There are several recipes, but try this one. First beat the roe till creamy, add a little flour and salt and make into small dumplings. Drop them into boiling well salted water (or sea water). They will rise to the top when done. Eat hot or, when cold, slice and fry in butter.

liver koogs

(baked potatoes stuffed with fish liver)

Wash large, baking potatoes but do not peel. Hold each potato longways and core (use an apple corer). Do not make a hole at both ends. Fill the potato centre with fish liver and put on a greased tin. Bake in a moderate oven 2 hours. Cod liver is very oily and this is balanced by the potato very well.

The Hollanders found, by long Experience, that this mighty Shoal of Herrings have their grand Rendezvous about the Middle of June near Braffa-Sound . . .

herring

When buying, choose herring with bright eyes. Gently press above the vent to tell if the fish has hard or soft roe.

fried herrin'

Herring is oily; it needs only flour and seasoning. Scrape off scales, wipe and remove head. Split up the back (from tail to head). Cook dry in a hot pan (wash it out before it cools).

For 6:

2½ lb fresh herring
1 lb onion, sliced

Wash and remove head and backbone. Melt a large knob of butter and fry onion and fish. Both should be golden brown and cooked through. Eat with boiled tatties.

Boiled herrin'

Pull off the head, do not cut. Scrape off scales, do not wash the fish. Cut across the thick back of the fish, nearly to the bone, before putting in boiling water. Simmer only 5 mins (for herring have only to see a fire and they are cooked . . .)

herrin' an tatties

Use a heavy pot. Layer sliced potato/herring/seasoning, starting and topping with a potato layer. Add a little water, put on lid and keep over a gentle heat. Both will be ready to eat together. Serve with plenty of butter, and a shake of pepper. Try salt herring this way, but soak first in milk.

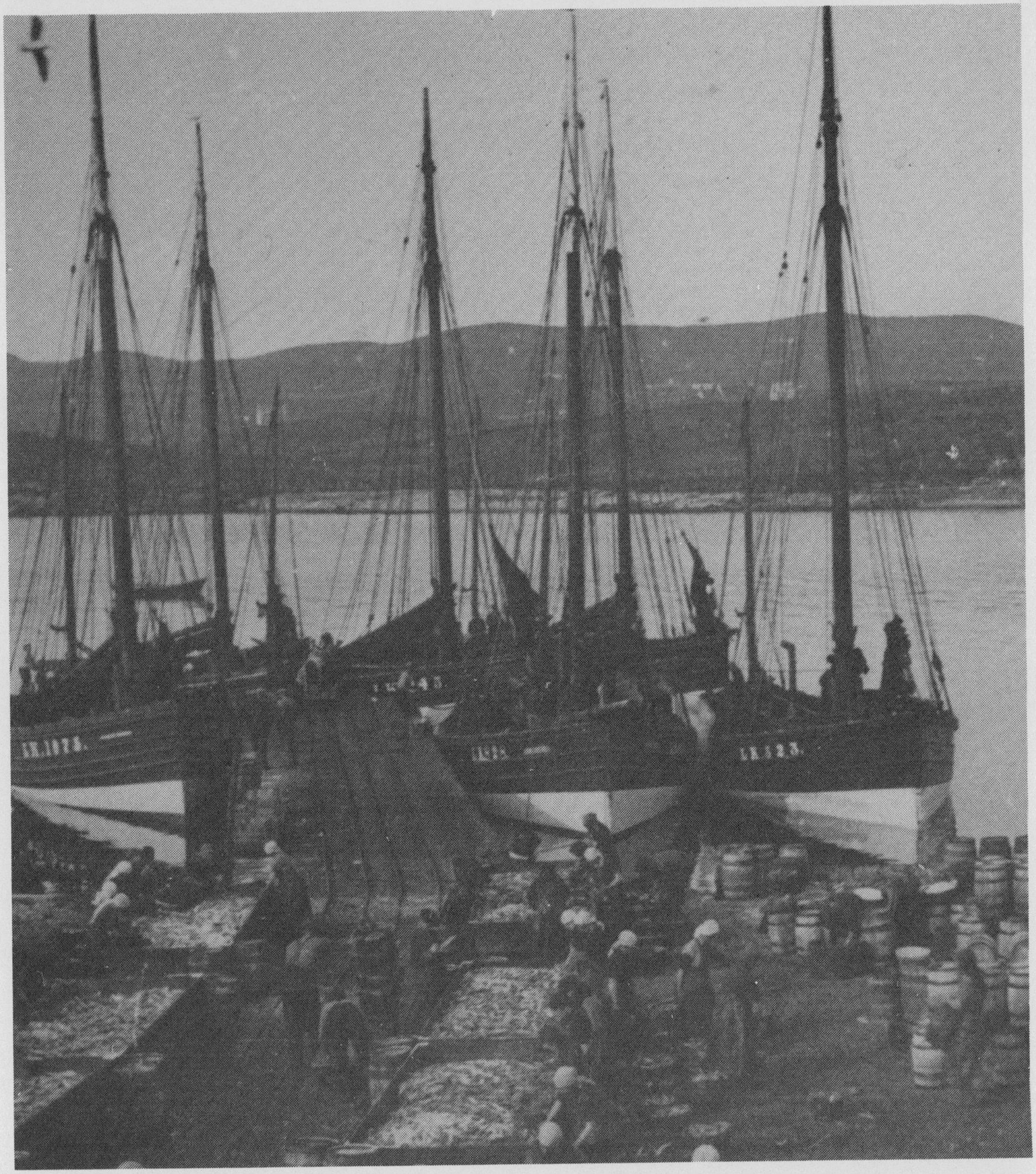

There has been feen at one time in Braffay-Sound 400 fails of Dutch Buffes employed in the herring fifhery, which is fo profitable a branch to that thriving nation.

potted HERRING

Split herring into 2, and with fingers remove the backbone (from head down to tail). Roll up and put together in a shallow dish, rolled sides up. Sprinkle with seasoning and cover with ½ water, ½ vinegar (or lemon juice). Cover dish closely and set at side of the fire (or in a moderate oven for 30 mins). These are delicious cold.

KIPPER

Kipper is brined, dried and smoked herring. Sometimes the fish are dyed whilst being smoked. These are reddish brown. (Undyed kipper looks yellow-brown). Choose kippers that are oily on the cut side (they come from fat herring). To cook, put in a large frypan and cover with cold water. When the water starts to boil, the kipper is ready.

Early in the 18th century some Shetland lairds exported herring to merchants in Hamburg, but the haaf was by tradition the more important. A hundred years later there was little change . . . 'the common people are very poor, and in the beginning of summer there is a great bustle in getting men to go to sea and fish the whole summer for their masters.' Not until late August were herring fished. By then, those which had not been caught by the Dutch had spawned — and once rich shoals were spent. The first yard for herring curing opened in 1826 at Lerwick. Soon there were others: beyond Grimister, on Bressay, Whalsay and the Skerries, at Scalloway, Levenwick and Cullivoe.

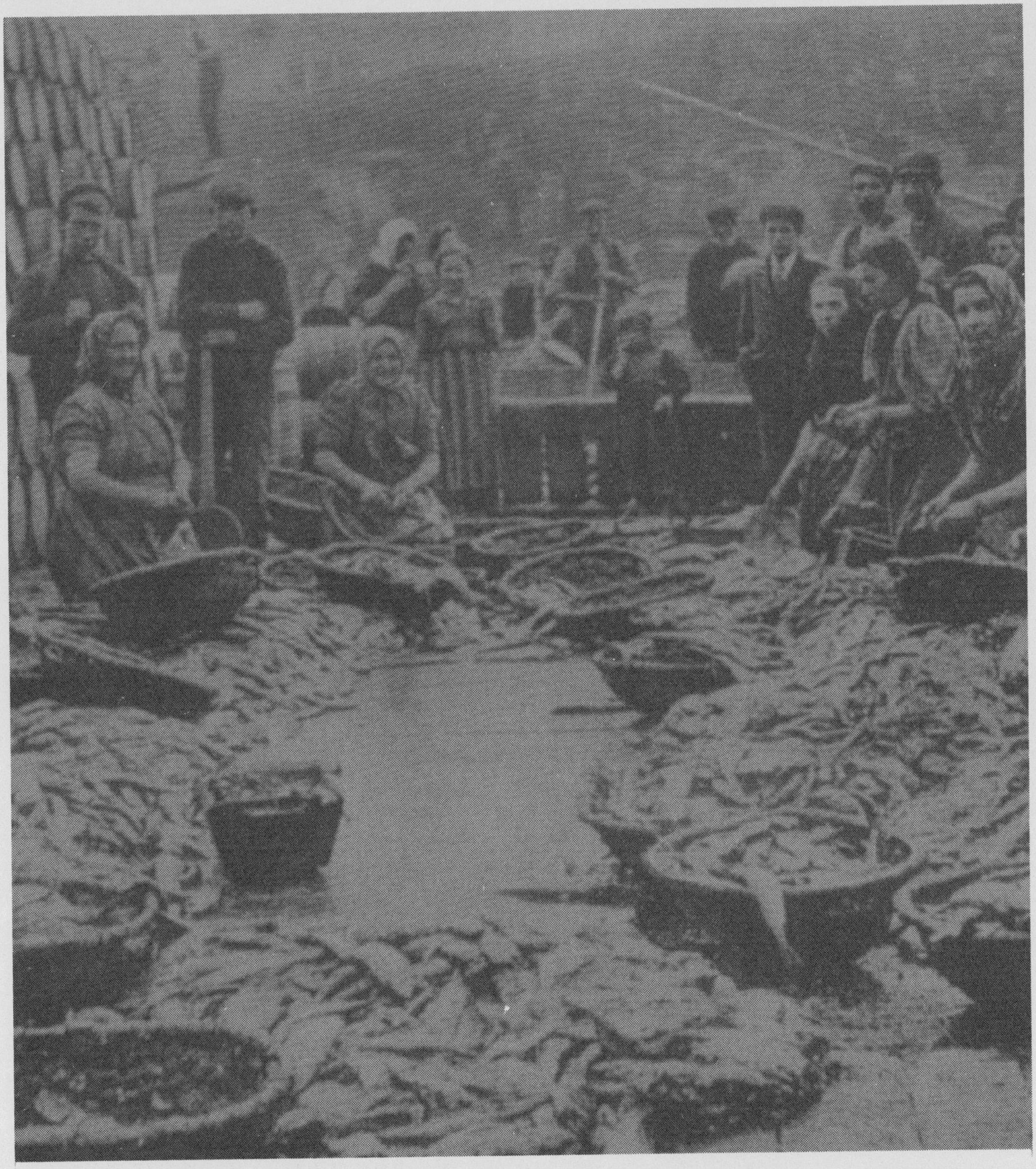

flats

include plaice, sole, flounder, dab. Available all the year round but with more flavour during the first months of the year. The easiest and most flavourful way of cooking is to steam. Put the washed fish in a lidded dish (or on a covered plate) atop a pan of boiling water — the fish cooks in its own juices. Eat with a little salt and plenty of butter.

skate

Skate is traditionally kept salted and dried for winter eating. It is a tough fish unless very young. Keep two or three days before eating, then scrub and soak for 1 hour. Cut the wings to a suitable size (each wing may weigh up to 2½ lbs) and put in cold water adding ½ teacupful vinegar for every 2 pts. Bring to boil, then simmer. The pinkish flesh will turn white when well done. Skin when still hot.

skate and liver

Cut wings into thick strips and roll round pieces of the fish liver. Tie. Soak in cold water before boiling. Eaten with jacket potatoes this is a good and filling meal for a winter day.

sea trout

Sea trout (or salmon trout) has a delicate flesh and its flavour is best brought out cold. Cook by poaching in water or bake, well buttered inside and out, in a moderate oven for 30 mins.

porpoise

. . . there is a part of the Creature which the natives eat . . . the finny part . . . and it seemed to me to resemble oxcheek . . .

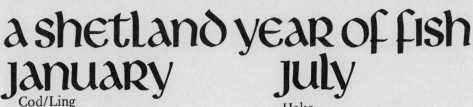

a shetland year of fish

JANUARY

Cod/Ling

Haddock   Flats
Hake   Whiting

FEBRUARY

Cod *(to early part of month only)*

Haddock   Whiting
Hake   Flats

MARCH

Halibut   Haddock
Hake   Flats
Whiting

APRIL

Halibut   Whiting
Haddock *(scarce)*   Herring *(late April)*

MAY

Halibut   Haddock
Herring

JUNE

Hake   Haddock
Halibut
Herring

JULY

Hake

Haddock   Mackerel
Halibut   Herring

AUGUST

Hake

Haddock   Mackerel
Whiting   Herring

SEPTEMBER

Mackerel *(early part of month)*   Whiting   Hake
Herring *(scarce)*

OCTOBER

Cod/Ling   Whiting
Hake   Torsk

NOVEMBER

Cod/Ling   Hake
Haddock   Whiting

DECEMBER

Cod/Ling   Hake
Haddock   Whiting

FROGRIE

Frogrie (Mackerel) is not good unless fresh. It is best caught and eaten the same day. If buying, choose only those fish with a clear eye and body marking.

To fry: gut and clean. Rub well-seasoned oatmeal over. Cook on split side first, and baste with oil and butter mixed. Try with gooseberry sauce (page 65).

Mackerel can be baked whole in the oven. First britch (score) with a knife. Dot with fat and seasoning. Cover well (or wrap in cooking foil) and put in a moderate oven for 15 mins.

Mackerel can be potted in vinegar like herring (page 32) but cut in short thick pieces rather than rolling up.

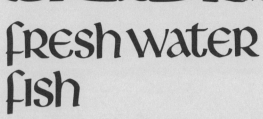

fresh water fish

If they smell muddy, soak in water and vinegar 1 hour. Scald if the fish is slimy, then rub dry.

eel

(One small eel is a meal for 2)

Eel is best in the months at the end of the year, when wintering eels return to the sea. Clean thoroughly and cut up. (Eel blood is poisonous if it can get into a cut or graze). Sprinkle with salt and leave to stand for an hour. Rinse before cooking.

To fry: use oil and butter, rolling the pieces of eel in seasoned flour first.

eel and potato

(for 4)

2 lbs potatoes
1 lb eel, cut in small pieces
salt and pepper

Slice peeled potatoes thin and layer with the eel pieces in a buttered dish with a lid. Season layer by layer. Pour over 1 teacupful thin cream. If lemon juice is added the eel will be very tender. Put on lid and cook in a smart oven 45 mins.

trout

Clean all blood off and remove gills (they give a bitter taste). Leave head on — when the trout is cooked the eyes turn white. Rub lightly with seasoned, fine oatmeal before frying or grilling. Have the grill very hot and cook each side about 4 mins.

salmon

(really a sea fish which breeds in fresh water)

The Scottish season is from early February to the end of August. If buying whole, choose one with a small head but heavy shoulders. The scales should be silvery. Allow 4 ozs per person as it is very rich eating.

It would be difficult to find a more industrious race than the Shetlanders. The men do the heavy work on the croft . . . the women . . . always doing the reaping and looking after the cows, which they take to graze on the hill, and sometimes even doing the ploughing; they knit perpetually; they carry peat and unload the boats . . .

Salmon is best cooked very simply. Put the fish in a heavy pan and pour warm, salted water over. Bring to a very gentle simmer. Allow 15 mins for thick salmon steaks, 10 mins per lb if the fish is less than 5 lbs, 8 mins per lb if it is over that weight. Cool in cooking liquid, but skin before the fish is cold.

shellfish

Shellfish are not part of the traditional Shetland diet: they were put on a hook rather than on the table. But Shetland shores can provide a delicious source of food — yours for the picking.

kroklins

Kroklins (mussels) are best October to March. Never use any that are already open, or any that open soon after being put in the pot. Allow 1½ pints of mussels per person. First wash and scrape shells and put in a heavy pan. Heat, shaking the pot so they all open (mussels give out enough salt water, and taste best, when cooked this way). Take out, discarding any empty half shells, and put in a hot bowl. Reheat the cooking liquor, pour over and eat with plenty of bread to mop it up. (Look for tiny 'seed' pearls: they make Shetland jewellery).

winkles

Pick from below the tide line on a fresh coast. Keep in a bowl of seawater for 1 hour before cooking, to clean. Put a plate on top of the bowl or the winkles will walk. Boil 15 mins. Use a large pin to get them from their shells and eat with pepper and butter -- or with garlic butter (chop a clove of garlic, mix well in a small pat of soft butter).

Broon an green silliks, an red an black wilks fur wis.

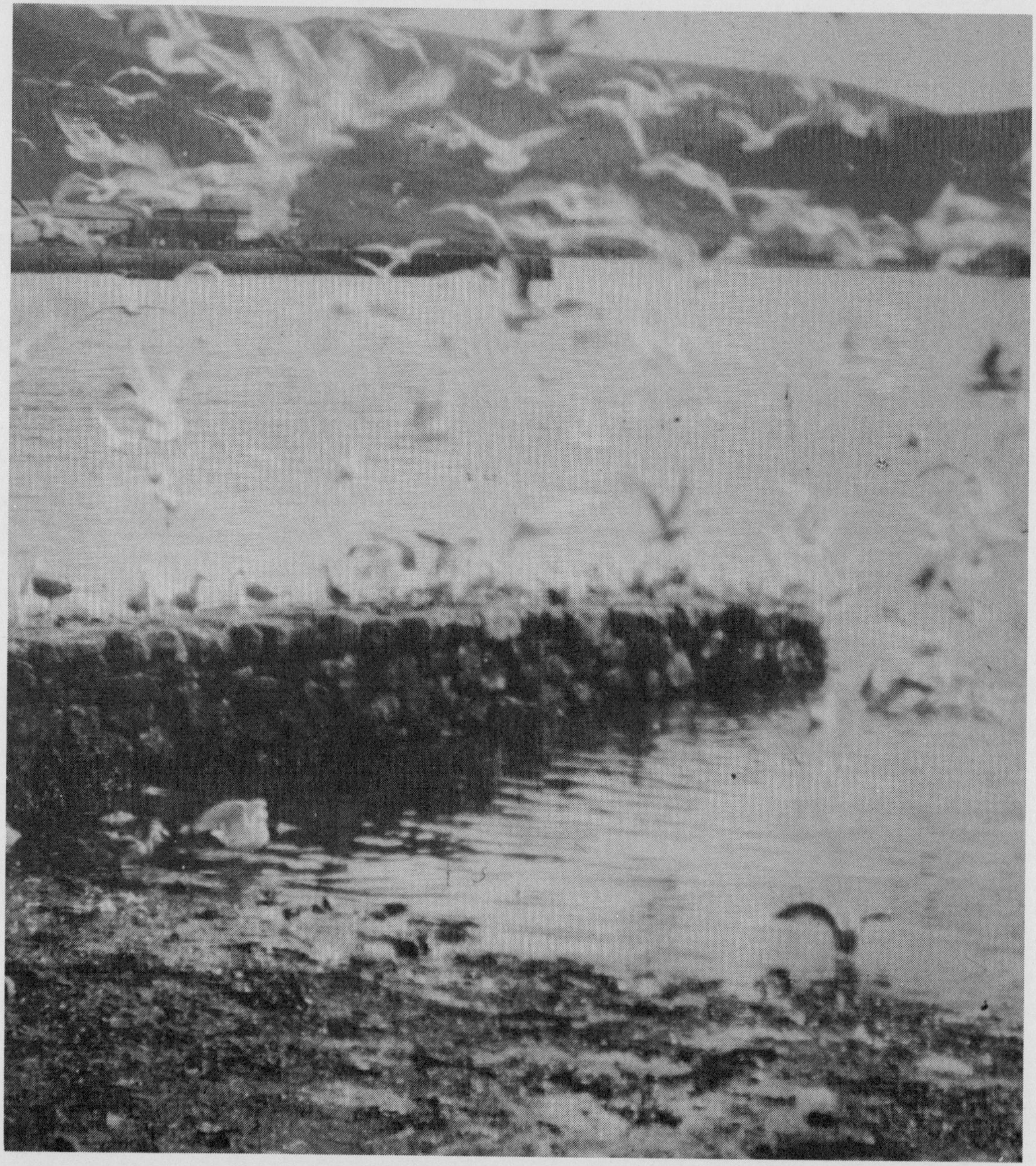

scallops

When fresh, scallops have a bright orange roe. Heat in a pan till the shells open, cut through the hinge and lift the scallop off. Do not use the dark parts, but cut the rest into bite sized pieces. Simmer gently a few minutes, drain and add salt and pepper. Eat with butter from the half shells, which are fireproof and can be kept hot. Scallops are delicious in a fish stew or soup but do not let them cook too long.

spoots

Spoots (Razor shells) are hard to catch. Dig for them on a clean sand beach at the edge of the lowest tide line. Cook like scallops.

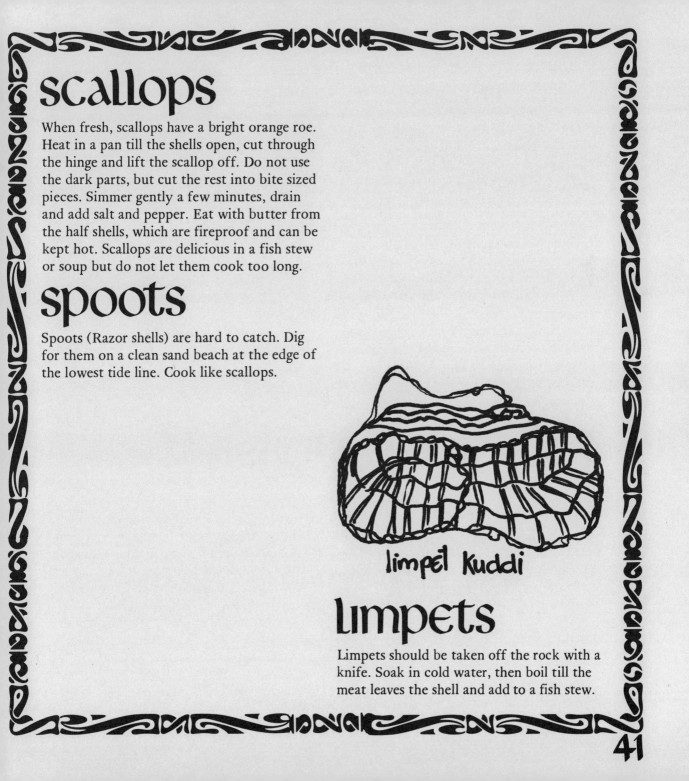

limpet kuddi

limpets

Limpets should be taken off the rock with a knife. Soak in cold water, then boil till the meat leaves the shell and add to a fish stew.

CRAB

By law, a crab must be over 4½ inches across
the shell before it is sold. Choose one that is
heavy in proportion to its size. Wash well,
remove any seaweed and fill any holes in the
shell with bread. (The bread will swell and
prevent the meat from becoming waterlogged
during cooking). Drop in boiling salt water and
cook 15 mins. When cold break off claws and
take out the body. Throw away the green
parts, stomach and gills. Both brown and white
meat are eaten, but chop separately and pile on
the crab shell. Eat with warm, buttered bannocks.

Crab is best during May and until September.

LOBSTER

Lobster must be 9" long before it can be sold.
Choose one which is between 1½/2½ lbs, and
alive. If buying a lobster ready cooked, the
tail should spring back when pulled out straight.
Tie claws and drop in deep, boiling water, head
first. Hold lid down. Simmer for 12 mins per
lb. If it is to be eaten cold cook for 10 mins
and leave to cool in the pot. Take out and
drain (make a hole in the head). Split the
body and remove the black intestine and head
sac. All the rest of the meat can be eaten. A
wire — knitting needle — is ideal to take out
the claw meat.

GRAINS

BRUNNIES

(Norwegian brun — brown)

4 teacup wholemeal flour
1½ tsp salt

and 1 tsp baking soda and 1¼ cream of tartar
buttermilk

or 2 level tsps baking powder
sweet milk

Add a teaspoonful of sugar if afforded . . .

Add buttermilk or buttermilk substitute
(page 61) to make a soft dry dough of all the
ingredients. Turn on to a floury board and
roll out lightly about ½" thick. Cut in quarters.
Have the girdle ready and wipe over with fat.
If it smokes the girdle is too hot.

A back is the wooden bowl for dough making.
Mellins is meal kept specially for dusting
over the bannocks.

stir with the right hand,
turn the spoon
with the sun and the
way of the seasons.

Five or six families co-operate in the building
of a mill, and they may become its owners a
few days after the foundation-stone has been
laid. Their wives, when they wish to grind a
peck of corn, turn the rill against the wheel,
and sit by the stone with a peat or two burning
on the floor, and tea in preparation, perhaps,
till the rough process is completed. After
grinding the grain the husk is sifted out of the
meal by hand . . . previous to grinding . . . it
is dried in a kiln (built into the family barn),
well trodden in a basket while still warm, and
then winnowed between two doors.

43

girdle (griddle)

BRUNNIES OF RYE *(Old Norse — rugr)*

¾ breakfastcup flour
¾ breakfastcup rye flour
¼ tsp baking soda
a knob of butter
buttermilk (about ½ pint)
a pinch of salt

Melt the butter and pour into the flours and add salt. Stir the baking soda into the buttermilk and add. Work to a stiff dough.

A good spoonful of molasses gives a delicious flavour though it is not a traditional ingredient.

SWEET MILK SCONS

2 breakfastcup white flour
butter size of an egg
1 tsp sugar
sweet milk
2 tsp cream of tartar with 1 tsp soda
(or 1½ tsp baking powder)

Sieve flour, soda, tartar (or baking powder) and salt. Add sugar. Rub in butter lightly with fingers. Mix with sweet milk to make a soft dough. Roll out ½" thick, cutting into ▭'s. Bake on a girdle or the middle rack of a quick oven till brown (10-15 mins).

OATMEL GRUEL

(for 1)

An omik o' mel, steepit ower weel. Het til hit glaanses dan tak wi' a grain o' saat.

Soak a good cupful of oatmeal overnight in cold water. Then cook till it turns thick, stirring. Eat with a pinch of salt and a wooden spoon.

bere

Bere . . . is regarded as the most important corn crop, being sown on the best land.

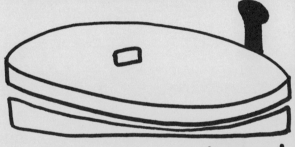

haand quern

BURSTIN

Burstin is bere corn which was dried at the fire in a pot till roasted and then handground, using a quern. It made a rich brown meal.

You canna whistle an aet burstin.

BURSTIN GLUG

This is traditionally made with burstin and water (or milk or buttermilk) eaten raw.

GLUG

This is made by stirring uncooked oatmeal into cold water.

KLIND KRÜL

This is burstin knead into a thick cake, cooked over the fire.

KRÜL

A krül is a sma' bannock of oatmeal and water with butter put inside or spread on top. Take as a mid-morning 'piece'.

BERE MEAL GRUEL

Bere meal makes a thin but creamy porridge
with a slightly nutty flavour. For 4, bring 3
breakfastcupfuls of water to the boil. Stir in
the meal slowly, cooking all the time. It is
ready in 10 mins (do not add too much meal).
Try with a knob of butter and a sprinkle of
salt instead of milk or sugar.

*Mill-gruel is made with milk. It is extra rich
and was traditionally kept for special feast
days, such as Johnsmas in mid-summer.*

BERE MEAL BANNOCKS

1 breakfastcup flour
1 breakfastcup bere meal
1 tsp baking soda and ½ tsp cream of tartar
1 dssp butter
buttermilk

*Add in a dssp of good treacle for a richer
bannock.*

Melt the butter (and treacle, if used) and pour
into the meal, flour and salt. Put the soda and
tartar in a cup of buttermilk, so they are well
mixed and frothy, and add to make a light
dough. More buttermilk can be used, as
needed, but do not let the dough become
sticky. Knead lightly on a mealy board,
making medium-sized bannocks or quarters.
Bake on a girdle, then toast slightly in front
of the fire. When cooked but not cooled rub
in bere meal. If the bannocks are set to cool
together under a cloth they will be soft.

blaanda bread

Blaanda meal (bere and oatmeal mixed and sown together) was used to make blaanda bread.

Here is a recipe to try —

1 teacup bere meal
pinch salt
sweet milk to mix
1 teacup oatmeal
1½ tsp baking powder
marg or vegetable fat the size of a large hen's egg.

Rub fat into the meal mixture, salt and baking powder. Add milk gradually, using the right hand. The dough should be firm, not sticky. If too much liquid is added, balance it with bere meal (and add a little more baking powder). Shape it into a round flat bannock and bake slowly on a girdle.

A snoddie is a thick bannock, baked slow in the ashes of a peat fire. Now bere is hardly cultivated at all in Shetland, but there is a mill in Orkney.

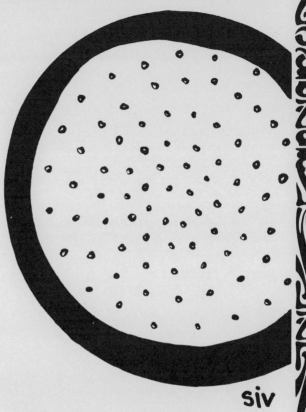

siv

There are only two public mills in the whole of the county of Shetland, one at Quendale . . . and one at Girlsta . . . although there are the remains of many old water mills to be seen . . . hand mills or 'querns' are still found to be in working order.

47

wooden
bale

VIRPA
OR SOO'ENS

This can be made by steeping the sids (unhusked oatmeal) in water. This is seda-soop. Cover and set in a quiet, warm place, stirring once a day. The fermented liquid is swatts; it makes a pleasant drink. The longer it is kept fermenting the more acid it will taste. Generally, keep at least ten days but the steeping will be much shorter in warm weather or if warm water is used. The soo'ens can be strained off and fresh water added either to start more swatts or cooked as a thin, creamy gruel. When food was especially scarce this was an important way to conserve stocks of grain, the swatts a useful substitute for milk. Until early this century it was common for a lump of soo'ens rolled in oatmeal to be taken as a 'piece'.

The sma' oat was grown commonly in Shetland . . .'it is a little, small, hungrie, leane Oate' . . . which withstood high winds and thrived on the poorer soil of the outfield. This is the Bristle-Pointed Oat, a species of wild oat, but by the early 1800's was cultivated only in Shetland, Orkney and on the higher parts of central Scotland, all areas with difficult climate and soil.

STOORADRINK

Stir a little very fine oatmeal (stoor is dust) into swatts, until slightly frothy.

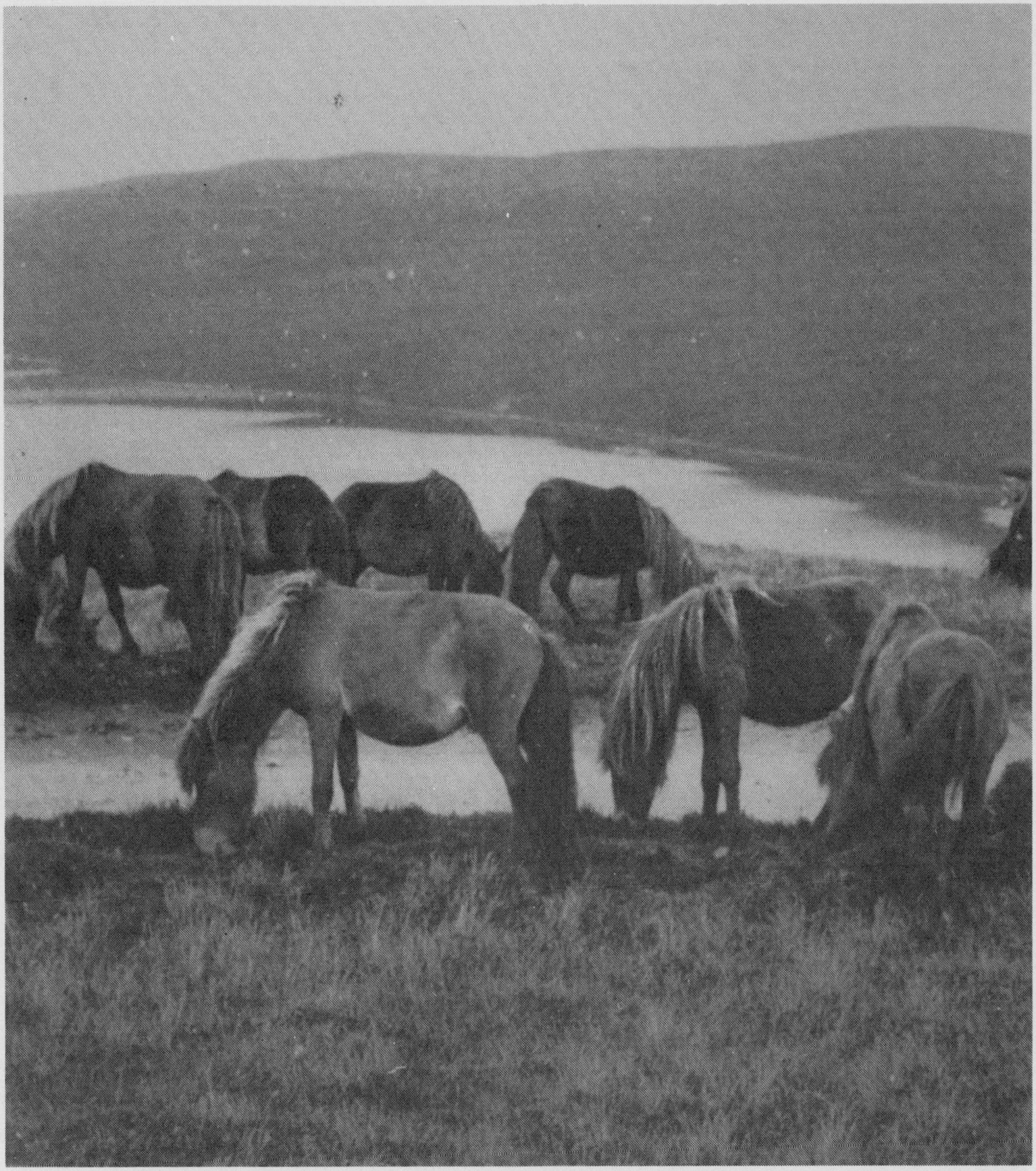

BRaand iRon BaNNocks

3 breakfastcup white flour
1 tsp salt
2 tsp baking soda and 1 breakfastcupful sour or buttermilk OR
3 tsp baking powder and 1 breakfastcupful sweet milk

Sift flour and salt and rub in a knob of lard (the lard will keep them soft). Add baking soda stirred into the sour/buttermilk (or baking powder in sweet milk) and mix to a dough. Divide into long bannocks and put on the braandiron (this makes a ribbed pattern on them) or greased baking tin in a hot oven (20 mins).

The meal would have been stored dry, in sheepskin bags.

fatty BRuNNies [oatcakes]

Oats were at one time the main cereal crop grown in Shetland, oat brunnies the 'bread' of the islands.

Use a medium oatmeal or two-thirds oatmeal to one-third fine flour. Add a good pinch of salt. Melt sweet dripping with water over a gentle heat, then stir in to make a moist mixture. A little whey will improve flavour. Work in the bowl with the right hand, till the mel sticks together, then turn on to a mealy board and knuckle into a flat cake. Roll thin and cut in △'s. Rub over with dry oatmeal before firing. Oatcakes are cooked on one side only, slightly brown, when they should be set on edge (upper side toward the fire) to harden. Oatcakes taste much nicer if they are warmed first. Try them spread with rhubarb jam (page 63).

A biddie is a thick oatcake which the fishermen took to eat at sea (sea biddies). Tivlachs are thick too, but made with coarse ground meal.

braand iron

buttermilk girdle scons [pancakes]

Iurnin' tree

1½ teacup white flour
1 tbsp sugar, if liked
¼ tsp salt
2 tbsps melted butter
2 eggs
½ tsp baking soda and 1 breakfastcupful buttermilk OR
1½ tsp baking powder and 1 breakfastcupful sweet milk

Beat eggs and buttermilk (or sweetmilk) and stir with melted butter into the dry ingredients. Have the girdle hot and wipe over with fat or cooking oil (if it smokes it is too hot). Put the mixture in tablespoonfuls (about 4 on the girdle at one time) to cook and turn when the bubbles rise to the top. Cool the scons in a cloth, to keep soft.

Their grain consists of oats, barley and rye.

tattie brunnies

These were made from potato flour (dried tatties, roughly ground in a quern).

1 breakfastcup mashed potato (or potato flour)
1 dssp butter
1 teacup self raising flour
pinch of salt

Mix mashed potato (or the flour) with butter Add salt and work in the self raising flour. It should hold together firmly. Roll thin, prick all over and cook on a hot well-greased girdle. Best eaten hot, with butter and a glass of milk.

Meal fed the men who built some of the first roads in Shetland in the mid 19th century. They were paid in maizemeal and not money, for a succession of disastrous harvests, hard winters and then potato blight had brought starvation and near ruin to many families.

vegetables

lentil brö

(for 8)

Put 1 lb lentils, teacup barley and 2 large onions, a carrot and neap cut small into the pot. Do not throw out onion skins as they give good extra colour to soups and stews. Boil up, then simmer for 2 hours. Add a good spoonful of meat extract or beef cube. Check for seasoning. This makes a meal with bere meal bannocks (page 46) and butter.

thick vegetable soup

(for 6)

4 breakfastcupfuls water and a large piece of beef dripping OR
4 breakfastcupfuls stock OR
4 breakfastcupfuls water with a chicken cube
½ large neap
2 carrots
kale
3 medium potatoes
2 onions or leeks
½ teacup barley
salt and pepper

Cut the vegetables in bite sized pieces and add to the boiling liquid. Let simmer slowly 1½ hours. A few mins before dishing add a tea-cupful of milk.

Traditionally, vegetables and meat or fish were cooked together in stews or soups. Often a handfu' of meal went in the pot too. It was simplest, when croft work took the women outdoors or when there was little time either for cooking or eating.

green pea soup

(for 4)

4 breakfastcupfuls ham stock (or boilings from a ham)
2 teacups marrowfat peas (soaked overnight)
salt and pepper

Simmer till soft. Put through a sieve and re-heat. Eat with warmed fatty brunnies (page 50).

nettle broth

Pick only the tops of young nettles. Use gloves! Wash under a running tap and put to a boiling stock with a handfu' of barley. Potatoes can be added, to thicken the broth. (Nettles cook like spinach — they 'shrink' — so pick a good basket-ful).

The weather is changeable, with damp and stormy winters, but summer in Shetland at its best is unsurpassed for mingled sunshine and bracing air.

tattie and oatmeal soup

(for 4)

Peel and dice 4 medium tatties. Add to 3 breakfastcupfuls water with ½ teacup coarse oatmeal. Simmer slowly. Taste for seasoning. This should not be a very thick soup, so add more water if necessary.

It is traditional to cook slices of reested mutton in the soup too.

neap

If large peel first and boil cut in thick pieces. It is good cooked slow with a little water, then mashed with butter and salt. (Neap burns easily so use a non-stick pan over a gentle heat).

In the early part of the year there are few fresh greens ready but stooins (the tops of young cabbage) are delicious if boiled a few minutes in a little water till tender and then covered with melted butter. Radish and neap tops can be cooked the same way.

pattern of crops

1st year	ley (fallow)
2nd	bere or oats
3rd	oats
4th	tatties with patches of neap or kale
5th	bere or oats

but on poor land

1st year	ley
2nd	oats
3rd	tatties
4th	oats

It was the lairds of Shetland who first grew the potato in the islands, sometime in the 18th century.

chappit tatties

Mash boiled and salted tatties well with the back of a wooden spoon. Add a little butter and milk if liked.

Some Shetland varieties: Shetland Kidney, Champion, the 'black tattie'. They are lifted at the hairst, stored dry. Some crofts keep a tattie-hoose. Shetland tatties crop well; needful too, since grain stocks were not usually sufficient for winter wants, then dried tatties were hand ground to make a rough flour for baking tattie brunnies (page 51).

tatties-in-the-pot

The traditional pot is heavy, with a wooden lid, and hung over a slow fire.

Peel and slice tatties. Layer (with a pinch of salt each layer) in a casserole or lidded flameproof dish which can be brought to the table. Add a little water. When ready the slices at the top should be dry and soft. Just before serving put over chopped parsley and mint mixed.

A Shetland word for potatoes is oorack.

potatoes with milk (for 4)

Peel 1½ lbs potatoes. Slice and put in a fire-proof dish. Add pepper and salt to 1 large breakfastcupful milk and pour over the potatoes. Cook in a bright oven 1½ hours. Potatoes cooked this way eat very well with fish.

in the 16th century Shetland kale was sometimes the staple winter food

The sturdy cabbages . . . grow like dwarf oaks.

kale an corn

Put some water on to boil with a soup bone and cut up a few leaves of kale (or strip them from the central stalk). Whilst they are cooking add a good handfu' of coarse oatmeal (traditionally, k-nockit corn or groats). Season and strain. Put in a heated bowl and pour over a little warmed cream.

A traditional evening meal, with bere bannocks (page 46). The kale is sown during August or September in the planty-krub, a rough circle of stone or peat. Next April the seedlings are transplanted to the kale yard nearer the house. It is thought that Cromwell's soldiers brought cabbage seeds to Shetland, in the mid 17th century.

cabbage

Shetland cabbage have good solid hearts. Peel off the outer leaves and quarter (make the first cut lengthways). Put in boiling water, salted, and boil rapidly till tender. Drain well and butter. Eat with fatty brunnies (page 50).

mushrooms

Mushrooms are found wherever there are horses, late in the year.

Mushrooms cannot be confused with any other fungi: they have pink gills under a creamy white cap. Small ones do not need to be peeled. Never cook mushrooms for more than a few minutes. Try with baked fish, roast chicken.

milk
cheese
Butter

At no stage in the traditional ways of making butter or cheese was any waste allowed. A rich collection of dialect names for these bye-dishes survives. Here are a few to try, although it is not possible now to make and taste them exactly the same.

KLABBA (junket)

Heat 1 breakfastcupful new milk till lukewarm. Add 1 tbsp sugar and when melted stir in a layt of yearning (rennet) or a large sprig of butterwort. Stand bowl in a warm place till set, then put in a cold place. Delicious with honey.

A layt is just a little.

BLEDDIK

Bleddik is buttermilk, the liquid remaining after the butter has 'come'. It has a sharp taste. The whey is left to ferment, becoming clear and sparkling, a refreshing drink.

This is soor blaand. Kept in a small wooden keg it was taken by the crew of sixerns, far out at sea. Made regularly, it is the traditional thirst quencher (especially when working in the peat hill).

hevil daffik

kirn milk

Strain the buttermilk curds till dry, and eat with cream.

The curds would have been thickened by dropping a hot stone into the buttermilk.

blaand keg

hung milk

(simple cottage cheese)

Stand milk until whey and curds form. (A little lemon juice will 'turn' milk). Put the milk curds in a bag and hang to drip overnight. Empty the curds into a bowl. This is hard milk. Add a little sea salt. Chopped chives too. (Use the liquid which is left for baking).

ost-milk or usted

Heat sweet milk gently with a little run-milk (milk that has 'turned') or buttermilk. This makes a rich curd, like hung milk.

In Shetland, cheese was rarely made. Gammel-ost is old cheese.

A Shetland word for milk is skubba. Ewes were milked too, and the 'sheep-milk' used for butter and cheese.

kleebie

BUTTER

To make butter stand the milk two or three days till thick (soor milk). Then kirn till almost separated. Kirnin' stanes, kleebies, are dropped in to hurry the butter. Kirn again until the butter floats on the top. Wash it well using wooden butter pats. Salt butter keeps fresh longer.

TO CURE BUTTER

2 parts of the best common salt as fine as can be had. 1 Part of Sugar and 1 Part of Saltpetre beat them up together mixing well and then take 1 ounce of this for every 16 ounces of Butter beat it well and let it stand one month before using well closed up.

Both milk and butter are stored in kitts, wooden containers with close fitted lids.

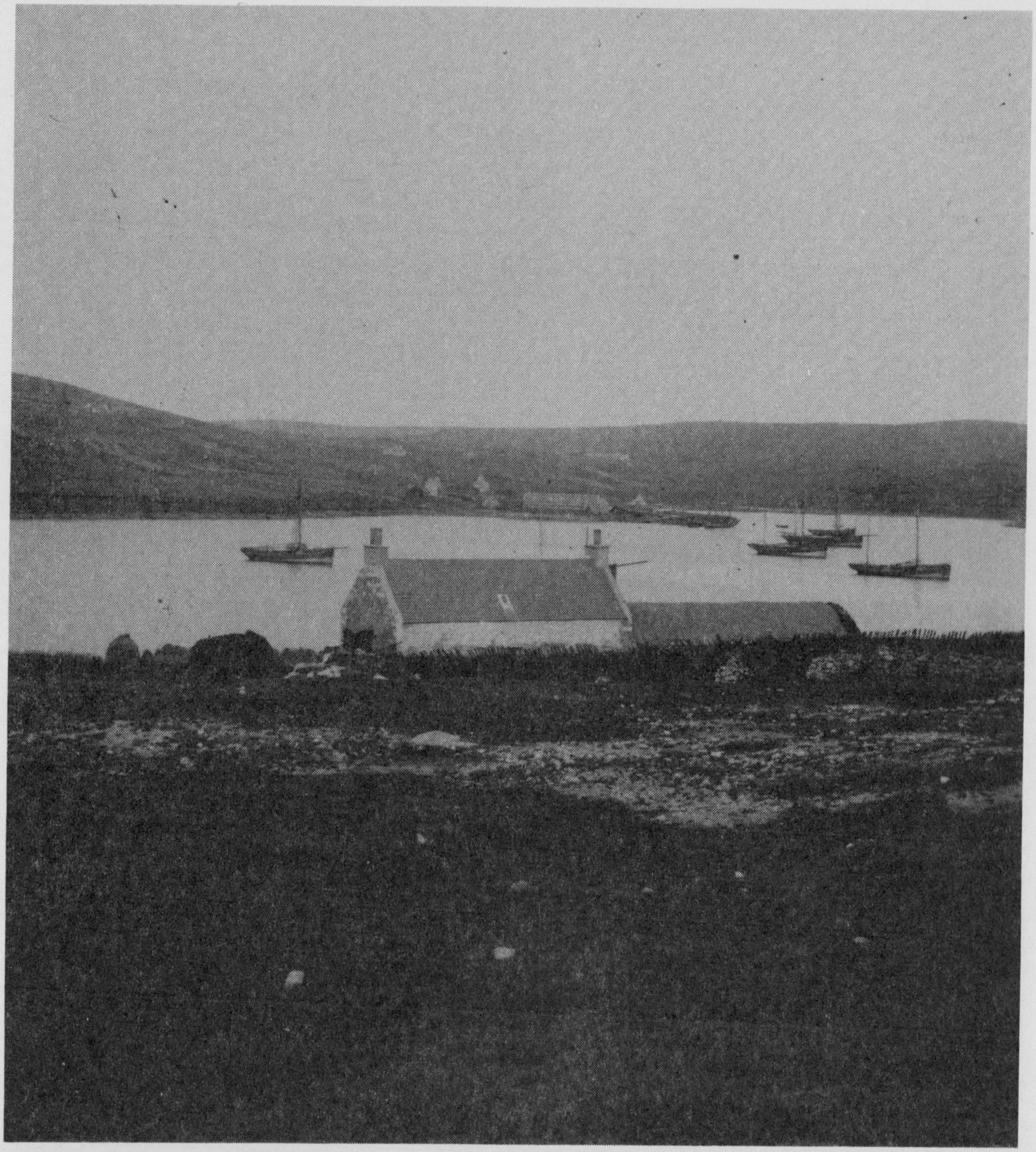

milk kug

Shetland butter, when carefully made, is equal to that of any country; but when made in part payment of rent . . . the quality is bad to a proverb.

Tho' these Islands are well adapted to feeding of goats yet they do not keep them, not finding them of advantage.

klokks (clotted cream)

Stand new milk for 12 hours so the cream rises to the top. Then heat to boiling point, and leave to cool. Skim off the klokks. Eat with cinnamon sugar.

strubba

Leave milk to separate, then strain off the curds. Mix with cream to make a thick but light mixture. Try as a topping on stewed or fresh fruit.

goyla

Goyla is whey with hot water mixed, to float the curds.

pramm

Traditionally made with burstin (page 45) and cream, milk or buttermilk.

Warm a little bere meal, do not let it burn, and fold into thick whipped cream. Try atop fresh fruit salad.

milk jelly

½ teacup carrageen moss, soaked in warm water (take out any bits that are black)

Put the carrageen in 2 breakfastcupfuls of sweet milk and simmer 30 mins. Strain. Add a little sugar and a pinch of salt. Leave to set. (Carrageen is also called Irish Moss and can be bought).

substitute buttermilk

Keep a few potatoes peeled and cut covered with water overnight. Put the liquid only in a jug and when it has turned sour use instead of buttermilk for baking.

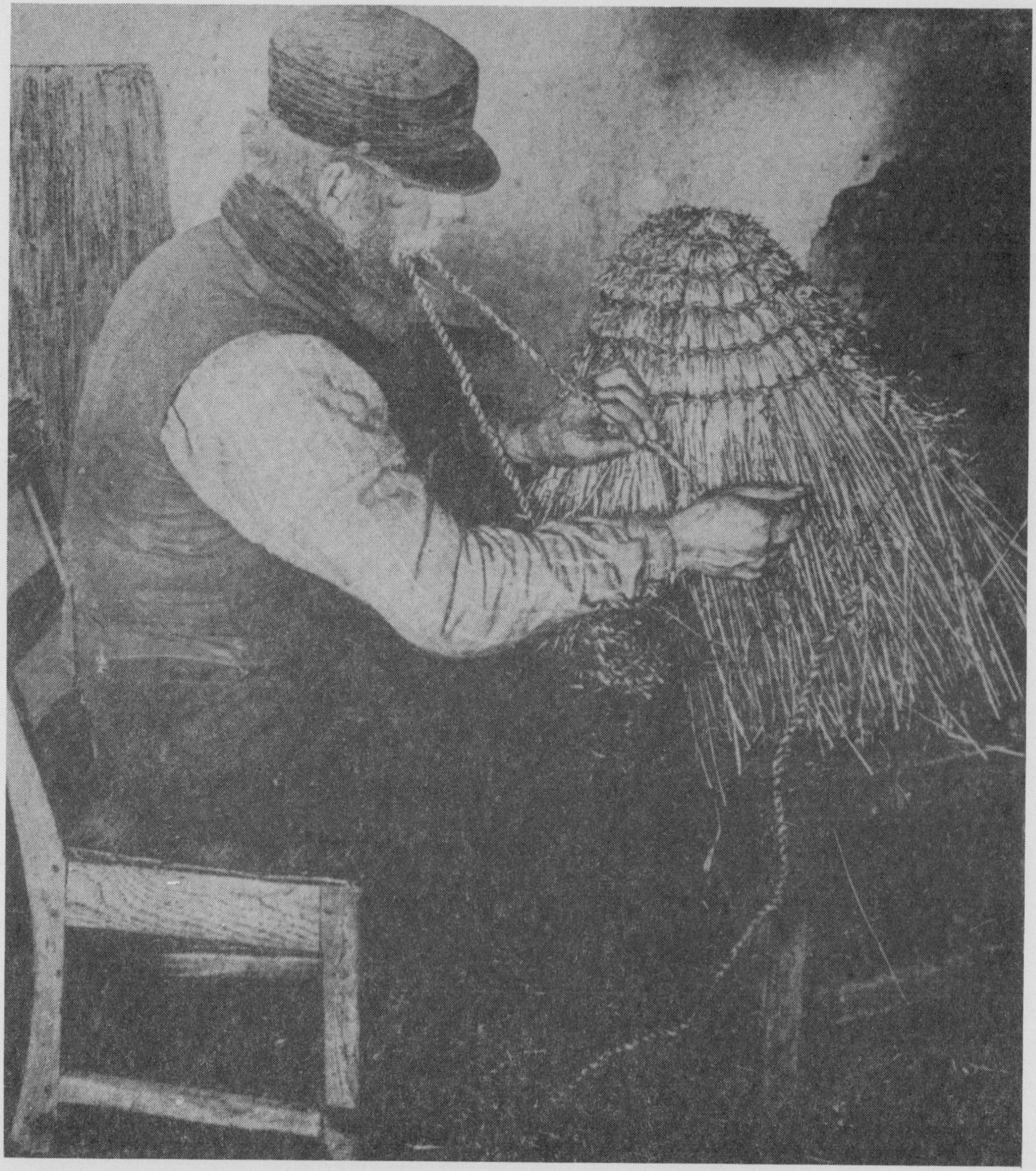

jams
sauces
pickles
relish

The recipes in this section are for the fruit and vegetables which have always grown best in Shetland.

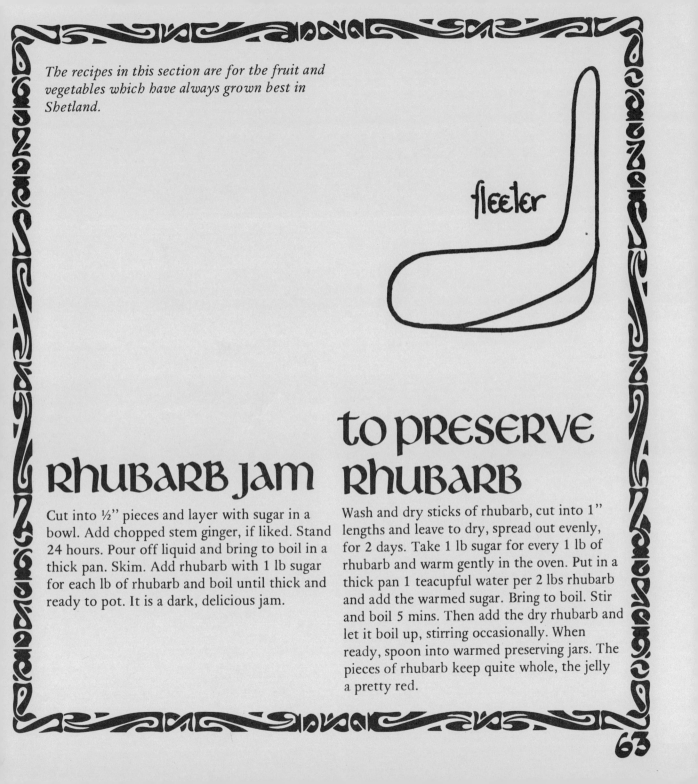

fleeter

RHUBARB JAM

Cut into ½" pieces and layer with sugar in a bowl. Add chopped stem ginger, if liked. Stand 24 hours. Pour off liquid and bring to boil in a thick pan. Skim. Add rhubarb with 1 lb sugar for each lb of rhubarb and boil until thick and ready to pot. It is a dark, delicious jam.

to PRESERVE RHUBARB

Wash and dry sticks of rhubarb, cut into 1" lengths and leave to dry, spread out evenly, for 2 days. Take 1 lb sugar for every 1 lb of rhubarb and warm gently in the oven. Put in a thick pan 1 teacupful water per 2 lbs rhubarb and add the warmed sugar. Bring to boil. Stir and boil 5 mins. Then add the dry rhubarb and let it boil up, stirring occasionally. When ready, spoon into warmed preserving jars. The pieces of rhubarb keep quite whole, the jelly a pretty red.

Bottled Gooseberries

This is an easy way. Take a large, wide-mouthed jar and fill with the cleaned gooseberries, adding enough sugar to sweeten them. Tie some paper over the top and set the jar in a pot with a little hot water in it. Put on the lid and leave to cook. The gooseberries will be beautifully tender but not mushy.

Rowan Jelly

(there are a few rowan trees in Shetland)

Pick clusters of fruit and trim off stalks. Cover with cold water, bring to boil and simmer till the fruits are soft. Pour into a fine sieve and leave to drain overnight. Next day add a breakfastcupful of fine sugar for every 2 breakfastcupfuls of liquid with the peel of a lemon (rowan needs extra pectin to set). Boil till the jelly forms and put in warmed jars.

Blae or Bilberry

To be found on Shetland hills in August and September. It is a very juicy fruit and does not need any water when cooking. Just cover with sugar and simmer. Add lemon juice, or boil with lemon peel, to set.

GOOSEBERRY SAUCE

1 breakfastcup 'top and tailed' cooked
gooseberries
(or 1 tin)
1 teacup butter
1 tbsp sugar

Put the butter and sugar to melt. With a fork
press the fruit through a large holed sieve. Boil
all together for 2 or 3 mins (stir all the time).
The sauce should not be sweet as its sharpness
complements the oiliness of roast pork and
fried or grilled mackerel.

Lerwick contains about 25 hundred people;
out of which are seventy-five shopkeepers,
who deal in everything from fish-hooks to
herring nets . . . Eggs 1½d. per dozen, butter,
6d. a lb.; mutton, 2d. a lb.; fine oysters 4d. a
100, large cod fish 3d.; potatoes, 2d. a peck;
a fowl, 4d., duck, 6d.; goose, 1s.

pickled onion

Use 1 lb small onions (shallots are best). Peel
and leave in brine 24 hours. Then drain off
and boil 5 mins in fresh water mixed with a
little milk. Lift out and when cool put into
jars or bottles. Boil 1 breakfastcupful white
vinegar with 1 tsp pepper (white pepper if it
can be got) and pour this over the onions.
Cover when cold. Ready for use in a month.

trivet

BEETROOT RELISH

Boil beetroot without peeling or bruising the skin — twist the leaves off. When cooked and cold, peel and chop. Boil up white vinegar (allow 1 breakfastcupful per lb of beetroot) together with sugar (½ teacup per lb of beetroot) and sliced onion, if liked, for 15 mins. Add beetroot and cook a further 15 mins. Bottle and seal when cold. Hold the beetroot on the end of a fork when peeling, then it cannot stain the hands.

heather tea

First gather sun-dried flowers of heather then pour boiling water over and leave to infuse before adding honey.

RHUBARB RELISH

(it is a vegetable, after all)

Use malt vinegar, a large cupful for every 1lb in weight of rhubarb with brown sugar (allow 1 breakfastcup for each 1 lb of rhubarb). Orange peel and chopped apple should be added in, as liked, with a little salt. This is quickly made. Cook rhubarb, apple and orange peel till soft. Cool and remove the peel. Boil the vinegar and sugar smartly, then mix in fruit to heat through. Pot, covering when cold.

GREEN tomato RELISH

1 lb green homegrown tomatoes
3 large cooking apples
1 lb sugar
1 tsp ground cloves
3 large onions
2 breakfastcupfuls vinegar
salt and ½ tsp pepper
1 tsp ground cinnamon

Slice the tomatoes and stand overnight covered in salt. Next day put in a heavy pan with peeled, cored and sliced apples, sugar, onions, chopped, vinegar and spices. Simmer till soft. Bottle when cool and keep stored in a dark place.

feasts

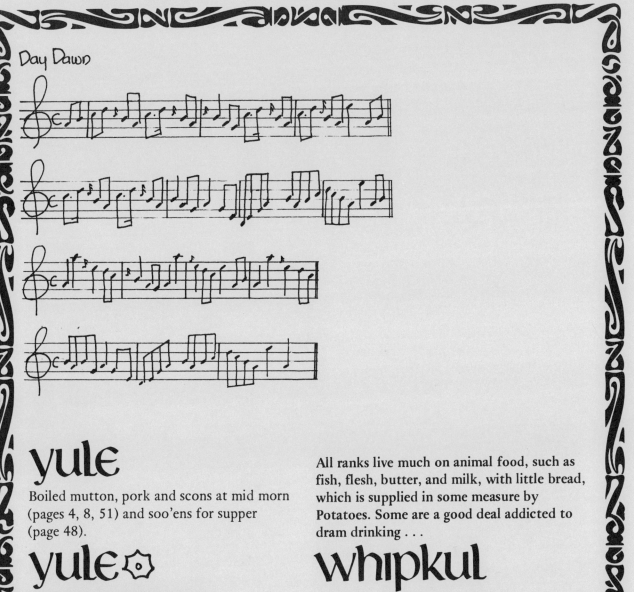

Day Dawn

YULE

Boiled mutton, pork and scons at mid morn
(pages 4, 8, 51) and soo'ens for supper
(page 48).

YULE ⊛ BRUNNIES

One is made for each member of the house.
Shape into points, like a star, with a hole in the
centre (page 43).

All ranks live much on animal food, such as
fish, flesh, butter, and milk, with little bread,
which is supplied in some measure by
Potatoes. Some are a good deal addicted to
dram drinking . . .

WHIPKUL

Beat egg yolks with sugar till thick and creamy.
Then add a good measure of rum.

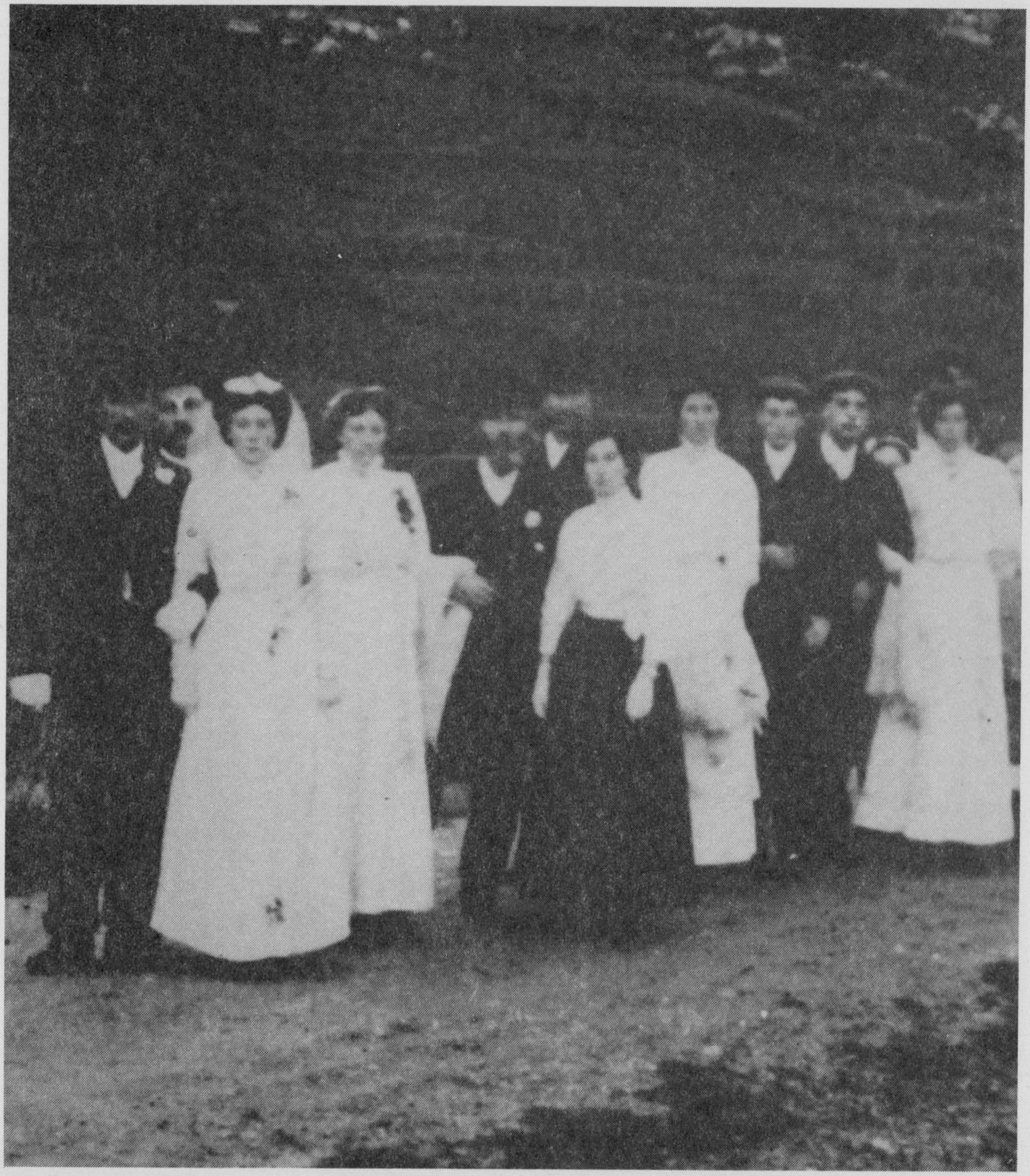

WEDDINGS

BRIDE'S BONN

By tradition, this is broken over the bride's head as she comes into the house for the first time as a 'mair'id wumman'.

Bride's Bonn, bridal cake, uses flour, fat, carraway seeds and, if possible, sugar. Take a teacup of flour with a knob of butter, a sprinkle of sugar and a thumbful of carraway seeds. Rub in the fat and mix with milk to make a soft, dry dough. Bake on both sides using the girdle.

CHILDBIRTH

EGGALOORIE OR CAADEL

Break eggs into a pan with a little milk and salt and stir till thick. Be cautious to smell each egg before using, for a bad one would spoil the whole.

This was given to callers visiting a mother and her new born.

69

mickalmas

A time of fresh mutton, black oatmeal puddings and burstin made from the crop newly ta'en in (pages 4, 10, 45).

up-helly-a

Up-Helly-Aa celebrates the end of Yule. A celebration too of the end of dark winter days, the threat of hunger over them. It is a time joyous to all, as the sun strengthens to the coming voar.

gruel tree

index

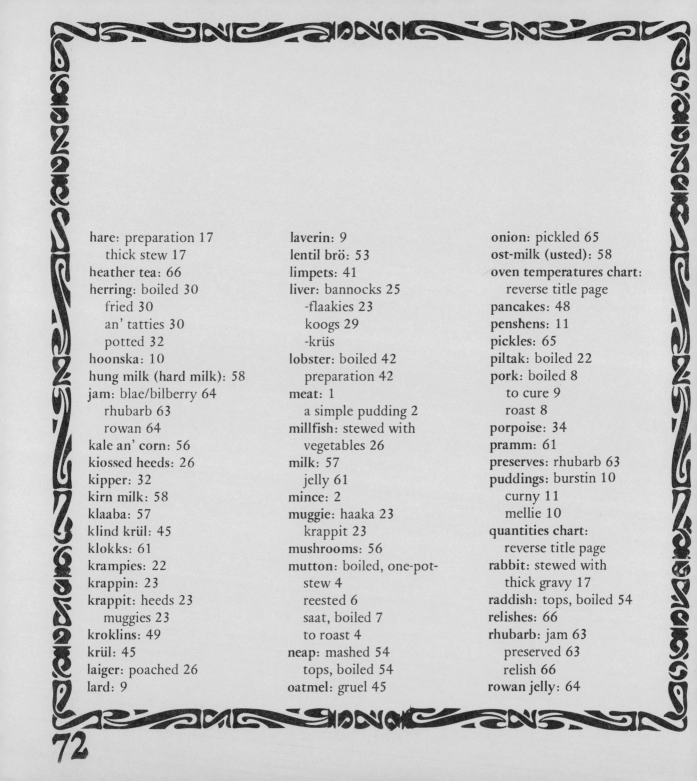

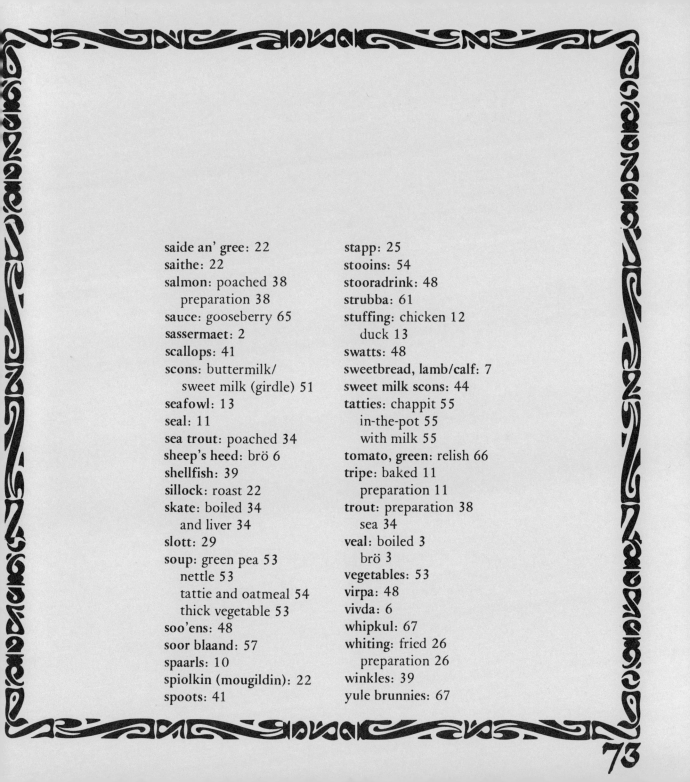

picture credits

All photographs not otherwise credited are from the author's collection.

Cover: Croft House, Dunrossness, c.1900
Title Page: Croft, Burwick, near Scalloway, c.1890
Contents Page: East Voe, Scalloway, c.1890
Page 1: Shetland ponies (Enlarged postcard ref: 5945 CWW [Williamson?]) c.1900
Page 3: Man with cows, c.1920
Page 5: Sheep rooing (Postcard, C J Williamson, Scalloway) c.1930
Page 7: Shipping lambs for market, Grutness, Dunrossness (Postcard, W Leslie, Dunrossness) c.1908

Page 11: Scousburgh, looking West (Postcard, J D Rattar, Lerwick) 1934
Page 13: Kittiwakes and guillemots (Postcard, J D Rattar, Lerwick) c.1930
Page 14: Croft and yard c.1880
Page 15: Spiggie Loch, Dunrossness (Postcard, T&J Manson, Lerwick) c.1910
Page 16: Men with dogs and guns, c.1910
Page 18: South Gio, Unst (from glass plate ref: 11141 JV [Valentine?]) c.1880
Page 19: Stenness Fishing Village (from glass plate ref: 10897 JV) c.1880
Page 21: Craigs fisherman, c.1890
Page 24: Return from the fishing (George Washington Wilson collection, Aberdeen University Library) c.1900
Page 27: Fishermen's huts, Fedaland (from glass plate ref: 10893 JV) c.1880
Page 29: Drying fish, Sound, Lerwick (from glass plate ref: 10873 JV) c.1880
Page 31: Fishing station, Lerwick, c.1870
Page 33: Herring workers, Lerwick (Postcard, Abernethy, Lerwick) 1903
Page 35: LK 880 in full sail, c.1900
Page 36: Lerwick boats and crew (from glass plate) 1905
Page 38: Bringing home the peats, Unst (from glass plate ref: 11133 JV) c.1880
Page 40: Pier, Westshore, Scalloway, c.1900
Page 43: Corn mill, Scalloway, c.1880
Page 46: Shetland crofters winnowing corn (Postcard, Valentines) c.1900
Page 49: Shetland ponies on the cliffs (Postcard, Schwerdtfeger, London) 1910
Page 52: Mail carts leaving Lerwick, c.1880

quotations

1635 English Husbandman Markham *(page 48)*

1733 Historical Description of the Zetland Islands Gifford of Busta *(page 8)*

1751 A Voyage to Shetland, the Orkneys & the Weftern Ifles *(title page, pages 2, 18, 30)*

1774 A Tour thro' Orkney & Schetland Rev. G. Low *(page 67)*

1775 Account of the New Method of Fifhing on the Coasts of Shetland Jas. Fea *(page 28)*

1780 Journal Kerr *(pages 6, 51, 61 [bottom])*

1787 Considerations on the Fisheries in the Scotch Iflands — General Accot. Jas. Fea

1813 General View of the Agriculture of Shetland Shirreff *(page 61 [top])*   *(pages 20, 32)*

1831 A Walk in Shetland by Two Eccentrics *(page 19)*

1837 . . . Guide to the Islands of Orkney & Shetland Robt. Dunn, Animal-Preserver, Hull

1874 On the Agriculture of Shetland Evershed *(pages 43, 45, 56)*   *(pages 22, 34)*

1882 Black's Picturesque Tourist of Scotland *(end page)*

1920 Agriculture in Shetland M'Gillivray *(page 47)*

1920's Guidebook *(pages 26 [top], 54)*

1971 Shetland Fishing Saga *(page 32)*

1928 The Scotsman (Music) *(page 67)*

1962 Wi Lowin Fin Milne *(page 39)*

1977 The Shetland Times — Scalloway Notes J. R. Nicolson *(pages 26 [bottom], 42)*

1978 verbatim, 70 year old from Cunningsburgh *(page 10)*

Quotations not listed above are from sources unknown

Truly it is a withered
desolation — not a tree,
nor shrub, nor creeping
thing for miles and
miles. It is intersected,
nay almost cut in
twain at parts, by a
thousand sea-lochs . . .
and yet these pleasant
people smile upon it,
and call it beautiful . . .